Teacher education through classroom evaluation

Teacher education through classroom evaluation

The principles and practice of IT–INSET

Patricia M E Ashton,
Euan S Henderson

and

Alan Peacock

Routledge
London and New York

First published 1989 by Routledge
11 New Fetter Lane, London EC4P 4EE
29 West 35th Street, New York, NY 10001

© 1989 Patricia M.E. Ashton, Euan S. Henderson and Alan Peacock

Printed and bound in Great Britain by
Billings & Sons Limited, Worcester

British Library Cataloguing in Publication Data
Ashton, Patricia M.E. *1935–*
    Teacher education through classroom
    evaluation: the principles and
    practice of IT–INSET
    1. Great Britain. Schools. Teachers.
    In service training
    I. Title II. Henderson, Euan S. *1941–*
    III. Peacock, Alan, *1942–*
    371.1′46′0941

    ISBN 0-415-03212-1

Library of Congress Cataloging in Publication Data
Ashton, Patricia M.E.
        Teacher education through through classroom evaluation : the
    principles and practice of IT–INSET / Patricia M.E. Ashton,
    Euan S. Henderson, and Alan Peacock.
            p.   cm.
        Bibliography: p.
        ISBN 0-415-03212-1
        1. Teachers — Training of — Great Britain — Case studies.
    2. Teachers — In-service training — Great Britain — Case studies.
    3. Observation (Educational method) — Case studies. 4. Education
    — Great Britain — Evaluation. I. Henderson, Euan S. II. Peacock,
    Alan. III. Title.
    LB1725.G6A77   1989
    371.1′46′0941 — dc19   89-3495
                                                                  CIP

Contents

Contents

Contents

Figures and tables

Figures

Tables

Preface

This book is about the IT-INSET approach to improving children's learning. It argues that continuous improvement depends upon the quality of teachers' theorising about learning and teaching. Constructive theorising develops through skilled evaluation of learning and professional collaboration. It is suggested that these processes should pervade initial and in-service training and that teacher education is enriched when students, teachers and tutors teach, evaluate and theorise in classrooms together. IT-INSET (Initial Training - In-Service Education and Training) thus represents both a philosophy of teacher education and a school-based programme of collaborative evaluation.

IT-INSET began as a project funded by the Department of Education and Science and based at the Open University from 1978 to 1981. It continues nationwide, co-ordinated by the Centre for Evaluation and Development in Teacher Education at Leicester University School of Education. The Department of Education and Science has consistently supported the development, through its funding of the Centre from 1981 until the end of 1987. The Centre continues to co-ordinate the now well-established network of IT-INSET institutions and local education authorities.

In defining IT-INSET and describing and illustrating the evaluation of IT-INSET practice nationally in 1986/87, the book has two main purposes. It seeks to inform those in training institutions, local education authorities and schools who may wish to decide whether IT-INSET is a constructive development for them. It also seeks to contribute to the continuing improvement of IT-INSET practice by examining the characteristics of programmes in which the learning of children and adults is markedly enhanced and comparing them with those of less successful programmes.

The first chapter describes the theory and practice of IT-INSET and sets it within the current teacher education context. Part I (Chapters

2-7) consists of six case studies designed to convey the experience of IT-INSET from the perspectives of those involved in it in different capacities - as tutor, teacher, student, pupil, training institution IT-INSET co-ordinator and local education authority INSET co-ordinator. The case studies have deliberately been chosen to illustrate the potential of IT-INSET and thus to provide a yardstick for considering some of the difficulties which are described in the later chapters. Part II (Chapters 8-12) summarises the findings of the national evaluation of IT-INSET. Chapter 8 explains the considerations which influenced the evaluation strategy and sets out the procedures and instruments that were used. Chapter 9 reviews the evidence of the quality of IT-INSET practice in 1986-7 and defines four levels of achievement. The evidence concerning the benefits of taking part in IT-INSET to all involved is brought together in Chapter 10: increasing benefit is associated with higher levels of achievement. Chapter 11 establishes that different training institutions enjoy different degrees of success in IT-INSET and examines the characteristics of institutions, and of their partnerships with local education authorities, which result in more and less successful programmes. The identification of factors associated with more and less successful IT-INSET is continued in Chapter 12, focusing on the influences of tutors, headteachers and the IT-INSET teams themselves. The concluding chapter briefly reviews the philosophy and purpose of IT-INSET and suggests that while the programme is demonstrably effective in enhancing the learning of pupils and adults, it could be so to both a greater extent and more consistently. It is argued that, if IT-INSET is seriously adopted in any training institution or local authority, then decisive action needs to be taken. The chief constraints upon reaping the maximum benefits from IT-INSET are examined and a way ahead proposed.

This substantial collection of information about the operation of IT-INSET owes its existence to the continued sponsorship of the Department of Education and Science. The permission of the Controller of Her Majesty's Stationery Office to reproduce and adapt Crown copyright material here is gratefully acknowledged. In addition, thanks are due to officials of the Department of Education and Science and to Her Majesty's Inspectorate for their support throughout the project.

The effort devoted to IT-INSET is incalculable. At a modest estimate, over two and a half thousand students and tutors joined teachers for more than two thousand days to work with upward of eleven thousand children in 1986/87 alone. As the following pages show, there were very few who did not consider that time well spent in terms of benefits to adults and children alike. It is to be hoped that this book is some testament to all of that energy and professional endeavour. Many of the participants also consented to being observed and interviewed, responded to questionnaires and kept diaries. Many did so as a result of their commitment to developing IT-INSET and the book is an appreciation of their dedication.

The project has been well served by Michael Preston, a member of the Centre team from 1981 to 1985, and by Graham Impey from 1985 to 1987, who also contributed the analysis of the questionaires to training institution principals and to chief education officers. Many colleagues throughout the country have come to know the superlative efficiency of Molly Clitherow, Centre Secretary, and become familiar with her unfailing and reassuring presence at the end of the telephone. The debt to her personal standards in every aspect of a particularly complex role is immeasurable. Thanks are also due to Marjorie Richardson, who played a vital support role in the secretarial work from 1984 to 1987.

The national evaluation has been unusual in involving nine teachers seconded by their local education authorities to conduct studies of the programme in their own areas. They have been able to complement the national survey with specific depth and detail. The quality of their perceptions and their ability to capture the flavour of IT-INSET programmes and the opinions of those involved in them do much to bring to life the account which follows. Special thanks are due to Margaret Booth (Dudley), John Brooke (Calderdale), John Fenby (Leicestershire), Marilyn Finney (Birmingham), Diane Godwin (Essex), Terry Payne (Oxfordshire), Joy Rozier (West Sussex), Marion Smith (Leicestershire) and Philip Warren (Lancashire).

Introduction

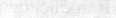

1

Introduction

In the words of Brian Cruickshank, In-service Education Co-ordinator for Leicestershire, quoted in Chapter 7 of this book:

> It seems self-evident that in-service education is about really meeting the needs of children through meeting the needs of staff ... [It should be] focused on what is happening in classrooms, what pupils are doing, and what teachers are trying to do with them.

The same can be said about the initial training of teachers. If this focus on what is happening in the classroom can be shared between practising teachers, as a form of in-service education, student teachers, as part of their initial training, and training institution tutors, an enormous potential is created for professional development.

That is what this book is about. In 1978, the acronym IT-INSET (Initial Training - In-Service Education of Teachers) was coined to describe an approach to teacher education which was designed to offer this potential (unfortunately before 'IT' came to refer to something quite different). IT-INSET has subsequently involved thousands of students, teachers and tutors in teaching in collaborative groups and in jointly evaluating the learning of their pupils. For nine years, the Department of Education and Science has funded the dissemination of the IT-INSET concept and the evaluation of its practice; that funding finished at the end of 1987.

In essence, IT-INSET involves groups of about six student teachers and a tutor forming a team with a classroom teacher (primary or secondary) for half a day or a day per week for at least a term. They focus upon an issue chosen by the teacher and each week, as a team, plan the work with the pupils, teach, observe and then subsequently discuss the pupils' responses and learning.

Perhaps the nature of IT-INSET may best be conveyed, at the outset, by an example rather than by an abstract definition. The following summary of her experience was written by Verity Gair, a team member who took part in an IT-INSET programme with 8- and 9-year-old children in a primary school in 1987.

One team's experience

Theorising or thinking systematically and critically about what one is doing is fundamental at all stages in IT-INSET. It is essential for the class teacher to theorise before the start of IT-INSET in order to choose the focus for the team. The class teacher discussed her ideas with the school of education tutor, the headteacher and other members of staff before coming to a decision. She was influenced by the importance given to problem solving in various documents published by Her Majesty's Inspectorate and by the Department of Education and Science, as well as by evidence of increased motivation in pupils when she attempted the problem-solving approach. IT-INSET offered her the opportunity to extend her knowledge and understanding of this approach beyond the stage which she had been able to reach by herself.

The initial meeting with the team gave other members the opportunity to theorise. As a group with a wide variety of backgrounds we drew on a number of experiences, including some involving pre-school children, and raised the following questions.

- How do children learn from practical activities?
- What kinds of teacher intervention are most successful?
- How do we improve teacher questioning?
- How do we help children to raise questions and how do we answer them?
- How do children convey their ideas to each other?
- What are the differences between girls and boys?
- How do children work as a team?
- Do children take note of displays?
- What do children think they are learning?

We had some limited experience of problem solving in science and technology and felt that it would be useful for us to start with a lesson about building bridges that the class teacher had used successfully the previous year. We felt that it might be possible to develop the theme of strength and stability in future lessons.

We hoped that analysing our observations of the pupils' activity and learning would enable us to deepen our understanding of the problem-solving approach. The following six questions from *Curriculum in Action* (Open University 1980) were used to structure our thoughts.

1. What did the pupils actually do?
2. What were they learning?
3. How worthwhile was it?
4. What did we do?
5. What did we learn?
6. What do we intend to do now?

By constantly referring back to classroom evidence, our theorising took on a new dimension. We were forced to justify our value judgements and consider very carefully the implications for future planning. As one student commented:

> In the early stages I was really impressed by the fact that all the children remained on task ... but there's more to it than sitting back and saying, 'They're all working - isn't this fun!'

Theorising about the value of children's discussions led us to raise major issues such as:

- How is language internalised?
- What is the relationship between language and learning?
- To what extent can children think and learn without language?

As a result of this discussion one team member re-read, with renewed enthusiasm and understanding, aspects of an Open University course *Language and Learning* (Open University 1973) that she had studied several years previously. She said that sections of Bruner's and Barnes' work took on a new significance which she could now relate to real instances in the classroom.

From their various backgrounds, each member of the team was able to offer some theoretical knowledge that was relevant to our discussions. We were able to re-examine existing views and partly-formed ideas by reference to real classroom issues. This opportunity to examine existing ideas critically and systematically and put them to the test over a period of weeks in the classroom was seen by members as extremely valuable. It enabled team members to view external theory in a new light and to turn to it with enthusiasm. Thus in many ways the classroom experience and subsequent theorising acted as an ongoing advance organiser for turning to the literature.

Team members said that they found articles easier to read and more meaningful because they had a clearer idea of what they were looking for, and turned to a variety of different authors during the project. While external theory helped in the development of ideas, the classroom experience enabled us to view the literature more critically than we would have done previously. Gradually a cycle developed throughout the project that has subsequently been continued by the class teacher and some other members of staff.

Figure 1.1   The observation-theorising-teaching cycle

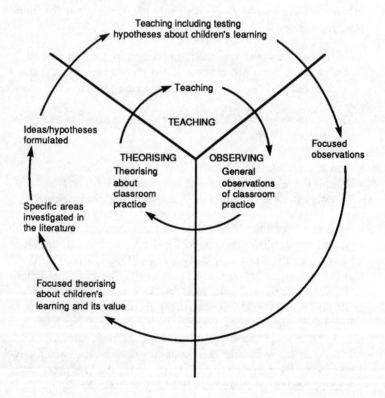

Teachers do make general observations of classroom activity and theorise about classroom practice, but usually without focusing their observations, turning to external theory, or putting their ideas to the test (the inner cycle in Figure 1.1). IT-INSET allows teachers the time to develop a more systematic cycle of focused observation, theorising, using published theory, formulating ideas, and putting them to the test (the outer cycle in Figure 1.1). This prevents empty theorising through which decisions are taken on the basis of insufficient evidence and are not put to the test.

We moved into the outer, IT-INSET cycle in Figure 1.1 when we began to categorise our observations in order to determine what the pupils might be learning. In the first instance we concentrated on three areas - language, behaviour in groups and problem solving. We drew up observation schedules and as a further but essential dimension we questioned the pupils after each teaching session.

We sought to improve the learning by providing opportunities:

- for group discussion and co-operation;
- to work with materials rather than on more abstract problem solving; and
- for planning and for children to modify and improve their designs.

We agonised over methods to assess what learning was taking place and eventually found a possible solution within *Match and Mismatch* (Harlen *et al*. 1977). The following week we continued to use schedules we had made ourselves for language and behaviour but added the *Match and Mismatch* criteria for perseverance, curiosity, open-mindedness, responsibility, originality, cause and effect and problem solving. Our observations gave us further evidence on how we could improve learning. Throughout the project our ideas developed on a number of issues.

- We felt increasingly that problem solving could not be an isolated activity, but that it is an approach that has to permeate the whole of the curriculum. We found that it helped if the teacher acted as a model, expressed doubt, hypothesised and, with the children, talked through problems that she had to face in the day-to-day life of the school.
- We came to realise that enabling the children to become involved in planning was crucial to the success of the problem-solving approach.

- In the early stages we had provided problems merely as exercises without enabling the children to take ownership of their own learning.
- We deepened our understanding of the process/content debate.
- We realised the value of assessing learning within the process skills and the value that this can be in matching.
- Working as a team enabled us to become much more objective, which is essential if theorising is really to benefit pupil learning.
- Mutual support enabled us to move forward more rapidly than we could have done by ourselves. As one student commented, 'We are able to take risks and make mistakes in a non-threatening situation, because it is a shared responsibility and we are all vulnerable.'
- Throughout the project we witnessed a narrowing of the gap which existed in people's minds between practice and theory.
- We realised the true value of our own theorising when it followed a systematic analysis of actual practice and the value of subsequently turning to external theory to consider questions we had raised about children's learning.

We used published theory in a number of ways. Questions raised in team discussions gave us a real purpose for returning to previous work done in degree and other in-service courses, often enabling us to see it in a new light. Sometimes we were inspired to search for answers within new sources. We were often surprised by the links between the literature on science, mathematics and language, particularly those of us who had only studied one subject in depth.

We used each other as resources and explaining our ideas to the rest of the team proved valuable for both ourselves and others. We realised that students are a valuable resource in INSET, a resource which is often overlooked. Theory encountered after IT-INSET was often seen in a new light. For example, the students were extremely interested in a session on different teaching styles later in their course. They were shown a video of how different teachers approached groups and the effects of this. We had raised this issue during our IT-INSET project from our own observations, and the students felt they had been more interested in it because of this.

We feel that the theory that many teachers take on board is that which they can relate to actual experiences in the classroom. Theorising with sympathetic and interested colleagues can deepen understanding and lead to searches within external theory, which in turn aids the development of ideas.

The principles of IT-INSET

The brief account above exemplifies the principles of IT-INSET, which may be more formally stated in the following terms:

In order to improve the quality of education provided in schools, teachers, students and tutors need to engage systematically and continuously in:
1. observing practice;
2. analysing practice and applying theory;
3. evaluating the curriculum;
4. developing the curriculum;
5. working as a team; and
6. involving the school's other teachers in the process.

The epistemological base which unites the first four principles is a definition of theory as intellectual process rather than as established knowledge. Thus teachers are seen to acquire professional knowledge through a process of practical theorising rather than by simply applying external theory to practice. The concept of 'theory' and 'practice' as separate entities is rejected and is replaced by one of theorising undertaken by anyone concerned with education. Teachers and others (psychologists, philosophers, researchers, curriculum theorists, and so on) have different degrees of access to classroom practice, different ranges of understandings, skills and expertise but, in essence, the process of theorising is the same for all. 'External theory' is defined, in this model, as theorising that is validated by reference to established principles within the relevant disciplines, is subjected to systematic testing, practical and/or intellectual, and is made public through print. It is an essential resource for teachers' practical therorising but not the sole source of their understanding.

Alexander (1984) proposes the following four assumptions which underlie this model of practical theorising and these are central to the IT-INSET concept.

1. Practice is inevitably 'theory soaked' and the teacher is inevitably a theorist.
2. Good practice is intelligent action validated by appeal to rational argument.
3. Theory for teaching comes from many sources - academic study, research, everyday experience - none of which can claim pre-eminence by virtue of its point of origin.

4. Theory for teaching is thus both the exploration and juxtaposition of existing theory, from whatever source, and the generation of individual theorising capacity.

The most significant feature of this model is that practical theorising is recognised as what teachers actually do; it does not imply that theorising is an unfamiliar activity in which teachers should begin to engage. This recognition establishes practical theorising as an integral part of everyone's teaching and not as an optional, additional activity. The assumption that teachers inevitably theorise is fundamental to the logic of IT-INSET as a form of teacher education. If teachers inevitably theorise, then a major function of teacher education must be to extend and support that theorising in three important ways.

1. Opportunities must be provided for teachers, intending teachers and tutors to articulate their personal theorising and to test out its logic in debate with others.
2. Skills need to be enhanced for gathering classroom evidence, for analysing it systematically and for reconsidering the value positions upon which interpretations and judgements are based.
3. External theory needs to be explored as a resource for practical theorising. The use of external theory and personal theorising, however, needs to be interactive. Personal theorising identifies questions or gaps in understanding where external theory may be of use. External theory may prompt new or modified conceptualisations of practice. In either case, personal theorising is needed to imbue the concepts of external theory with practical meaning and to test their contribution to developing understanding.

These activities form the substance of IT-INSET programmes. It is central to the philosophy of IT-INSET, however, that they should have the specific, consistent purpose of improving pupils' learning. Thus the gathering of evidence, the consequent theorising and the reconsideration of value judgements are used exclusively as means to the evaluation and development of the curriculum. The curriculum is taken to mean the entirety of pupils' classroom experiences and thus encompasses the syllabus or guidelines, the resources and organisation, the teacher's style, and the socal climate of the classroom. Given this definition of the curriculum, it follows that evaluation of the curriculum, and of the learning experiences which make it up, must be focused on pupils. Their learning and responses provide the evidence upon which evaluation of textbooks, schemes of work, teaching approaches, or classroom organisation must be based. To focus on teachers and resources alone, without regard to pupil response, is to deprive analysis of practical criteria.

Curriculum evaluation, and its constituent theorising, is context-specific, although not necessarily context-bound. Inevitably, practice and development of the relevant skills must take place within classrooms. IT-INSET is thus classroom-based. Nevertheless, generating principles for theorising which can be used in different contexts is intrinsic to learning to theorise more soundly and usefully. IT-INSET therefore combines the dual purposes of enhancing the learning of the particular pupils involved in a programme and improving the skills of all involved for future, independent use. In order that an IT-INSET programme will actually contribute to the learning of particular pupils, it is essential that it is the class teacher who will identify the issue with which the programme will be concerned.

The prime justification for the fifth principle of working as a team and, in particular, for combining teachers, students and tutors in teams, is the potentially enhanced quality of the work as different interests, experience, talents and perspectives are brought together. In addition, while most classroom evaluation is undertaken by teachers individually, its development is aided by the need to convey ideas and propositions to others and to accomodate theirs. Students and tutors are provided with an authentic experience of contributing to the development of pupils' learning and have the benefit of close collaboration with a classroom teacher. The teacher has the advantage of a group of outsiders committed to serving her or his purposes and supporting her or his endeavours. In addition, IT-INSET provides practice in teamwork skills such as communication, negotiation, compromise, leadership and collaboration, all of which are necessary if evaluation and development of the curriculum is to be a school-wide activity.

The sixth principle, concerned with involving other teachers in the school, establishes school-wide activity as the ultimate goal.

In these ways, IT-INSET is based upon a logically connected set of propositions which constitute a model for teacher education. The model can be practised with varying degrees of success. It can also be practised with a wide variety of different practical arrangements: team size, proportions of teacher/tutor/student members of teams, length of programme, time spent in discussion, year group of students, extent of additional INSET arrangements for teachers, source of the tutors involved, and so on, can all vary. The purpose of the programme, however, in whatever way it is practised, is critical. A change of intention from those described above, in any one of the constituent parts, invalidates the theoretical construct upon which IT-INSET is based. For example, any other role for the tutor than as fellow-learner and contributor, along with students and teacher, denies the concept of teachers as constructors of theory personally synthesised from different sources. Emphasis on students practising teaching with the guidance of teacher and tutor invokes an inconsistent apprenticeship model of teacher education. Any attempt to apply curriculum solutions, from wherever derived, without systematic attention to the evidence of pupil learning and response denies the intention to develop rational evaluation.

The partnership principle

The concept of partnership is currently much vaunted and has almost become a cliché. Nevertheless, IT-INSET does exemplify partnership between local education authorities, training institutions and schools. All that is meant is, first, that all three parties act in the knowledge that their prime concern is the enhancement of pupil learning and, secondly, that all three act in the knowledge that each has resources, experience and expertise that in combination will better serve the interests of pupils.

Though, ideally, IT-INSET would form a significant and continuing part of initial training courses, as yet it remains a relatively modest element, typically of half a day or a day per week for one term of the course. Even so, it is a means of establishing school- and pupil-focused discussions between local education authorities, training institutions and schools and can generate other forms of collaboration. At the least, it helps to develop common understanding of the educational task.

IT-INSET and action research

On first acquaintance, it may seem appropriate to classify IT-INSET as action research and to consider it to be subsumed by the 'teacher as researcher' model. Certainly IT-INSET has much in common with the central emphasis of action research on teachers engaging in a spiral process of making systematic studies of their classroom practice as a means to more securely founded action, which in turn gives rise to further enquiries. However, whether the IT-INSET approach constitutes action research, or whether it is similar but involves important differences, is much less certain. The debate only matters if bracketing action research and IT-INSET together obscures distinctive contributions that either activity may have to make to their joint concern with professional development and the enhancement of classroom practice.

Stenhouse (1975) substantially formulated the 'teacher as researcher' concept in the United Kingdom and much action research stems more or less directly from his work. Action research, however, embraces a range of activities, as witness, for example, the collections of studies by Nixon (1981) and, more recently, by Hustler, Cassidy and Cuff (1986). It is not always easy to disentangle common threads or to determine the precise meanings given to the same words by different writers. Indeed, Hustler *et al.* comment in their introduction that:

> The very compilation of this book has changed our own notions of action research, has left us unclear in places where we thought we were clear before, and vice versa.

These uncertainties are of particular moment when they concern issues on which IT-INSET takes a particular stance. In these instances, it does matter whether action research is really different, or only seems to be different because the points of similarity are implicit rather than explicit, or whether some individual forms of action research are similar while others are not. One point of uncertainty concerns the meaning given to the word 'curriculum'. Among writers about action research, meanings appear to range from substantial 'packages' of provision to all of pupils' learning experiences. For example, Tickle (1987), substantially following Stenhouse, argues that:

> The first need among teachers themselves is the recognition of curriculum as problematic.

This implies a meaning for curriculum that makes it possible not to see it as problematic and thus suggests something altogether much more remote than pupils' daily learning experiences. It seems inconceivable that all teachers do not see those as problematic and thus for IT-INSET 'the first need among teachers' is to recognise that more systematic attention to pupil response would be likely to make their actions more constructive. The latter interpretation of curriculum seems to be the one employed by Nixon and also Anning (1986), for example, both of whom regard themsèlves as action researchers. The definition of curriculum matters because it bears fundamentally on concepts of 'researching' it: enquiring systematically into a curriculum proposal places very different demands on a teacher from, for example, examining more closely the reasons why children ask her or him for help. Nevertheless, either study could give rise to important developments in classroom practice.

The concept of 'research' employed in action research is uncertain. For Elliott (1985) it seems to derive, at least initially, from a motivation to build bridges between the professional researcher and the teaching community. While he clearly argues for the role of classroom research in developing understanding of classroom practice, and thus in professional development, there seems to be a lingering flavour of research as an *additional* activity for *some* teachers. The emphasis on the requirement upon teachers to publicise their findings, and thus to move beyond the usual range of teaching activities in order to qualify as researchers, underlines this impression. This is echoed in Ebbutt's (1985) classification of teacher activity in British schools. Apart from the systematic collection of data and generation of hypotheses, the distinguishing feature of his 'Self-evaluation: action research mode' is writing reports open to public critique. This certainly seems to imply a concept of research far removed from that of teachers simply enquiring more systematically into their own practice which Anning, for example, would recognise as action research.

The relationships between teachers and outsiders seem also to be viewed differently in different forms of action research. The nature of those relationships is likely to be a product of the definition the partners give to research. Elliott's procedure of triangulation, for example, has some implication of the researcher (the outsider) and the researched (the teacher) and although the teacher is both willing and a contributor, the dominant frame of reference seems to be provided by the researcher. For Ebbutt, by contrast, an outsider is sought by the teacher and is described as a consultant or 'critical friend'. This appears to imply a more democratic relationship and a definition of action research which is closer to practical theorising.

The role of the re-examination of values in action research is also unclear. Stenhouse laid great emphasis on the development of professional judgement as an integral element in teacher research. But judgement does not figure explicitly in either Ebbutt's classification or Elliott's schematic representation of action research. Kemmis, on the other hand, does build evaluation into his cycle of steps in action research (Deakin University,1982). It may be that the issue of the value of classroom activities is implicit in British work. But it tends to be difficult to identify for certain and, without it, classroom enquiry can only give rise to fine tuning.

A crucial ambiguity concerns the exact purpose of action research. Some action researchers write almost entirely about the teacher and the improvement of classroom practice. Should an ultimate focus on the improvement of pupil learning be assumed? Or do teacher behaviour and classroom practice constitute a valid field for enquiry and do implications for pupils inevitably, or only possibly, follow? It may be significant that Hustler *et al.* conclude their introduction with the words:

> The action research movement is growing and, if the contributions in this book are anything to go by, the children in our schools seem to be benefiting from that growth.

Pupil benefit does seem to be incidental, rather than an intention. At the same time, there are undoubtedly self-confessed action researchers, such as Armstrong (1980), Rowland (1984) and Nind (1986), for whom pupil learning is the *raison d'être* of their activity.

Given this range of understandings, it is patently impossible to establish whether IT-INSET is action research. The most useful procedure seems to be to identify the defining attributes of the IT-INSET process so that others may judge whether or not it conforms to their understanding of action research.

The defining attributes of IT-INSET

1. IT-INSET is focused upon pupils' learning. Thus:

   (a) 'likely benefit to pupils' is the criterion for deciding whether or not to undertake a systematic enquiry; and
   (b) teacher behaviour is considered only in the light of its effects on pupil learning.

15

2. IT-INSET takes the curriculum to mean all of pupils' learning experiences and thus any enquiry into any aspect of the curriculum must focus on pupils' learning and behaviour.

3. IT-INSET assumes that all teachers theorise and its objective is therefore to assist in the improvement of theorising by practice in systematic data gathering, analysis and evaluation. Experience of these processes is intended to assist teachers in developing criteria for monitoring their day-to-day decisions, but it is recognised that they will only engage in them fully from time to time. It is as important for teachers to be aware of occasions when their decisions are inevitably based upon inadequate evidence or when their assumptions may be unfounded as it is to work fully through the processes of systematic data gathering, analysis and evaluation. Thus:

(a) the processes are appropriate for all teachers; and
(b) developing these processes is an imperative and not an option for teacher education.

4. IT-INSET takes the issue of values as central so that the worth as well as the effectiveness of pupil learning is examined.

5. IT-INSET encourages teachers to publicise their enquiries in order to contribute to, and influence, the collective development of understanding of classroom practice. This, however, is regarded as an optional consequence and not as a goal so that the failure to publish does not reduce the value of private enquiries. On the other hand, it is considered important to share enquiries, findings and reflections with staff colleagues so that, in the course of time, whole school staffs will collaborate in evaluating and developing the curriculum they collectively provide.

6. IT-INSET argues for the earliest possible and sustained opportunities for initial training students to develop their practical theorising, given its centrality in teaching and its role in making sense of external theory.

7. IT-INSET requires that tutors develop their practical theorising so that they constantly re-examine their own base in external theory and continuously resynthesise it with their own theorising, illuminated by that of teachers and students.

8. IT-INSET suggests that all of this is done most effectively when teachers, students and tutors seek to learn together from pupils whom they teach collaboratively.

IT-INSET and the national context

The last ten years, since the inception of IT-INSET, have seen an unprecedented flood of new policy and prescription relating to teacher education, both initial and in-service, from the Department of Education and Science and Her Majesty's Inspectorate. In this context IT-INSET can be viewed as a significant professional thrust.

IT-INSET patently contributes to meeting the Secretary of State's criteria for the approval of initial training courses (DES 1984), concerned with the involvement of teachers in initial training and the regular participation by tutors in classroom teaching. Moreover, it can be seen to meet the further criteria that:

Students should experience a wide range of teaching and learning methods and be given ample opportunity to discuss and assess them.

Opportunities should be provided for students to reflect on and learn from their own classroom experience, and to place their role as a teacher within the broader context of educational purposes.

Courses should ... pay attention to other aspects of the teacher's work, including the importance of staff collaboration in a collective professional approach to the curriculum.

[Training] Institutions, in co-operation with local education authorities and their advisers, should establish links with a number and variety of schools, and courses should be run in close working partnership with those schools.

[Subject studies should be conducted] at a level appropriate to higher education.

Indeed, the Council for the Accreditation of Teacher Education (CATE 1986) confirmed IT-INSET as a particularly effective approach to meeting the partnership criterion.

Equally, IT-INSET is an obvious means by which some of the aspirations expressed in recent documents published by Her Majesty's Inspectorate may be effected. For example, it provides experience for teachers and intending teachers relevant to participation in curriculum planning, curriculum leadership, and professional self-development, as well as to more frequent adoption of enquiry-oriented teaching styles (DES 1978, 1982, 1983, 1985). Most significantly perhaps, IT-INSET sits well with the concepts of teacher identification of INSET needs and evaluation of INSET in terms of professional classroom-related benefit, both of which are central to the Grant-Related In-Service Training (GRIST) arrangements (DES 1986).

However, whether or not any individual training institution or local education authority views IT-INSET as a significant development in professional practice depends crucially upon their existing philosophies. If local education authorities or training institutions view teachers as practical theorisers who cannot, by definition, merely transmit the national curriculum but who must interpret and elaborate it in the light of pupil response and professional judgement, taking the views of others into account, then IT-INSET constitutes a very serious option. If, moreover, they see effective teacher appraisal as including systematic evaluation of pupil learning and dialogue by teachers equipped with evidence of learning and rational argument, then again IT-INSET presents an entirely appropriate training experience. If they consider that teachers, with their combined experience and close working relationships with pupils and parents, must figure prominently in policy development, then clearly IT-INSET provides an ideal practice ground for teachers, intending teachers and those who teach them. If they believe that the identification of INSET needs, as required by GRIST, must be grounded in teacher evaluation of pupils' needs, then IT-INSET is not only a suitable means of gaining the requisite skills, but contributes to needs identification.

There are probably few who would dissent from such components of the concept of the effective teacher, and IT-INSET is an attractive option for many training institutions and local education authorities. The problem is that its attendant practical difficulties, the possible mismatch between its principles and current practice, and its radical and even threatening nature can too readily give rise to modified implementations which emasculate its potential major contribution to professional development. If this is not to happen, the contingent attitudes and arrangements must be consistent with the principles of

IT-INSET. In particular, the full implications of the concept of the teacher as a practical theoriser have to pervade practice in local education authorities, training institutions and schools, and this has wide implications for all aspects of initial and in-service education.

IT-INSET 1978-1987

IT-INSET was conceived by John Merritt, Euan Henderson and Derek Mortimer who jointly directed the original project, funded by the Department of Education and Science and based at the Open University from 1978 to 1981. As a result of the first national evaluation (Ashton *et al.* 1983), funding was provided for a three-year extension and the base moved to the University of Leicester where the enterprise was named the Centre for Evaluation and Development in Teacher Education. The main function of the Centre has been, and remains, the continued dissemination, support and evaluation of IT-INSET. In 1984, the Department of Education and Science renewed funding for the Centre. This funding ceased at the end of 1987, but the national network of IT-INSET training institutions and local education authorities has remained in being, managing its own dissemination and evaluation, and co-ordinated by the Centre with the support of the University of Leicester.

Throughout its life, the development of IT-INSET has been guided by successive Steering Groups, each composed of representatives of the Department of Education and Science, the co-directors of the original project, and members of the training institutions, local education authorities and schools involved. Their contribution has been invaluable in providing a broad base of interests and perspectives. The most recent membership is given in Appendix 1.

The numbers of training institutions taking part in IT-INSET has fluctuated throughout the project's life. Three were involved in the first year of the Open University project and the number had grown to twenty by 1981. In the subsequent six years, twelve of those withdrew and thirteen more became involved. The character of their involvement has changed significantly. Most of those who have abandoned IT-INSET depended on the personal enthusiasm of individuals or very small groups of tutors who took part with little or no institutional backing. Almost all those now taking part are doing so on the basis of institutional policy: their senior managements have figured prominently in the decision to adopt IT-INSET and in its subsequent implementation. In keeping with this shift of emphasis, whole-year groups of students are taking part as an integral element of their courses. The number of tutors and teachers involved have increased accordingly, as shown in Table 1.1. New interest continues to arise, and in 1988 there are twenty-seven institutions with established or planned IT-INSET programmes.

Many of the thirty-six local education authorities which have IT-INSET operating in their schools are taking a much more active part in the enterprise than hitherto. In some instances, IT-INSET is built into overall policy and is funded appropriately. Financial support takes the form of supply cover, travelling expenses for meetings, grants towards resources, help with printing and circulating reports, and replacing teachers released for short periods to act as IT-INSET tutors in schools other than their own and as evaluators. Advisers and officers are playing an increasingly significant role in actively supporting teachers' involvement in IT-INSET and in managing the overall development of IT-INSET in their areas.

Table 1.1   Number of institutions and individuals involved in IT-INSET in 1981 and 1987

	1981	1987
Training institutions	20	21
Local education authorities	17	36
Schools	88	285
Teams	132	440
Tutors	90	418
Teachers	169	639
Students	357	2108

The aim of this book is to reflect the nature and quality of IT-INSET as practised in 1986/87 together with the thoughts and opinions of those who, in a variety of capacities, have taken part in it. The evidence cannot, of itself, make the case either for or against IT-INSET and the gains made by children and adults as a *direct* result of the project defy measurement. Those involved have exercised their professional judgement of these gains, as must readers from the evidence which follows.

Part I
The Case Studies

The purpose of the case studies in Part I is to convey the nature of IT-INSET as an individual experience. Part II, dealing with the findings of the national evaluation, inevitably generalises about groups of participants and their experience of the IT-INSET process. The case studies complement these data by focusing on the experience, the learning and the reactions of a small cross-section of individuals. They describe what IT-INSET has meant to them as an element in their initial or in-service training, their classroom education, their tutoring role, or their wider responsibilities in a training institution or local education authority.

The first and longest case study (Chapter 2) describes the week-by-week experience of a team in a primary school. It sets out the elements of a typical IT-INSET programme and shows the initial decisions which need to be taken, the interactive pattern of classroom work and evaluation discussion, and the implications of genuine collaboration between tutor, teachers and students. The six-week programme was too short to achieve its full potential, but its brevity has made it possible to indicate the progress and conclusion of an individual project. Writing on behalf of the team, the tutor has drawn together the written and tape-recorded reflections of all its members.

Chapter 3 assumes some familiarity with the week-by-week pattern described in Chapter 2, and therefore provides less detail on the progress of the programme. This case study was written by the Deputy Headteacher of the junior school concerned and focuses particularly on his perception of the contribution of IT-INSET to teacher, school and curriculum development.

Chapter 4 combines selections from the written commentaries of teachers and students who took part in IT-INSET in a secondary school. All reflect on their expectations, their changing views as the weeks passed, and their assessment of IT-INSET as a part of their initial training course or as a form of INSET.

The fifth chapter reports briefly a survey of the views of 12-year-olds on their IT-INSET programme. The survey was conducted by a team working in a community college. The children comment on the education afforded them by the team and on the process of IT-INSET itself.

The next case study (Chapter 6) is written by the Director of Teacher Education Programmes at the College of Ripon and York St John. It describes the two years of planning which preceded the college's first IT-INSET programme and the evaluation of that programme. It serves to illustrate the range and diversity of responsibilities which fall to a college co-ordinator of IT-INSET.

The sixth and last case study (Chapter 7) gives the views of a local education authority INSET co-ordinator on the function of IT-INSET. He discusses its role in his authority's plans for teacher and school development, the practical and moral support which a local education authority needs to give, and some of the intricacies of collaboration with a training institution.

2

Sandfield Close Primary School

This case study was written by Peter Driver, the tutor-member of a primary school team which also included two teachers and five students. He draws on the team's minutes, his own notes, and tape-recordings of discussions. He has attempted to write on behalf of the team and to represent their shared perceptions of the experience: the team confirm that he has produced an accurate record. He provides a further dimension to the account by the addition of his own weekly reflections. In these, he exposes his anxieties about the role and responsibilities of a tutor in an IT-INSET team and highlights the elusive balance between, on the one hand, providing a team with freedom to determine their own progress and, on the other, allowing them to miss opportunities.

Sandfield Close Primary School has 425 children aged 4-11 and nineteen teachers, including the Head. It is located four miles north of Leicester. Over ninety per cent of the children are non-white, and many have English as a second language. The school was built on an open-plan design in the early 1970s. Additional buildings are planned, but at the time of the IT-INSET project there was acute overcrowding.

The class involved in the project was of 9- and 10-year-olds. The team consisted of the class teacher, another teacher from the school who normally taught in an adjacent area, five students and one tutor. Although the first time the whole team met together was on the first of their six IT-INSET days in school, contacts between team members had taken place earlier.

The five students had all been in 'partnership' at the school as part of their post-graduate certificate in education course. This involved pairs of students working closely with teachers for two days a week during the first term of their course. They were therefore all familiar with the daily routine of the school and had established good relationships with the staff and pupils. Indeed, two of them had worked with the class teacher and knew all the children.

The two teacher members of the team had attended a one-day meeting the previous term for the primary IT-INSET partnership teachers, at which they had met the tutor. A further meeting of the teachers and tutor took place a week before the project was due to start. It dealt with some of the practical problems involved, such as how supply cover was to be used and how eight adults could work in a very limited space. The students were on a block teaching practice and were unable to attend.

Before the first session in school, the tutor and students had only met once, on the students' IT-INSET preparation day. This included an activity in which the students were asked to observe a five-minute video of children working in a small group. They were asked to note down the things they thought the children were learning, and this was followed by a group discussion.

The main part of this case study is an edited form of field notes and a diary kept by the tutor during the six weeks of the IT-INSET programme. Each week is described under the headings of:

1. Planning and preparation
2. Activity
3. Evaluation
4. Planning

These sections are written from a team perspective without personal comment. They are each followed by a further section giving the tutor's personal reflections on the work.

Week 1: Tuesday 9 February

Initial preparation and planning In the first part of the session, the team discussed the elements of IT-INSET. Certain ground rules were agreed upon.

- A different person would chair discussions each week - their brief would be to try to ensure that everyone in the team had a clear understanding of the week's purpose.

- Another member would take and circulate minutes - these would act as a work agenda for the following week.
- The responsibility of the team, individually and as a group, was to work to enhance children's learning - the activities planned and the way the team organised itself should not jeopardise this.
- The team would share in preparation, teaching, observation and evaluation.
- In discussions, all members of the team would have equal opportunity to voice opinions and make comments, and all decisions would be made as a group.
- For each of the remaining five weeks the timetable would be as follows:

8.30 - 9.00 am	Preparation and planning
9.00 - 10.10 am	Teaching and observing in the classroom
10.30 - 11.30 am	Evaluation and reflection
11.30 am - 12 noon	Planning for next session

- To help focus and re-focus the work, there should be a statement of what was being looked at - this would be redefined if necessary.

So far, the team had not talked about which area of children's learning would be the focus of the project. The class teacher set the context. The junior part of the school had begun to review spelling as part of language policy. A system of using cards as part of a spelling workshop had been replaced by a text which the children worked through at their own level. There was concern about the children not checking their work and thus not correcting mistakes that they might recognise.

The members of the team then spent forty minutes with the children in the teaching area. They were able to see them at work with the text, learn some of their names, and become accustomed to the area. There was no structured observation.

The team decided that it would like to see samples of the children's work to form a base for future reference. It was agreed that a short extract, selected from a comprehension book, should be dictated to the whole class. The children would then continue the story from the end of the dictated passage.

Activity The class was already organised into four groups (not based on ability). The team worked in pairs, each with a group of seven or eight children. One team member dictated the passage while the other observed. Both then helped the children as they wrote their stories.

Evaluation The children's work was read and the team shared observations they had made. Some time was spent recording and analysing mistakes made in the dictation, although the mistakes found in each group were not discussed on a class basis or among the whole team. The work was not marked. The final few minutes of the meeting were spent in producing an agreed statement of the team's focus: 'Looking at the strategies used by children to improve their spelling.'

Planning It was decided that self-correction would be the following week's activity.

Further reflections on Week 1

The ease with which we began and continued to work together was in part due to knowing one another before the programme started. Students and teachers talked and listened to each other with confidence and respect. We quickly established the feeling of being a team. This was good, as the brevity of this IT-INSET programme, only six weeks, meant that there was little time to team-build.

We spent as much time discussing the ground rules by which we would operate as we spent with the children. This paid dividends for the following five weeks. We established a pattern of working which:

• gave the team an internal discipline - we always knew what we should be doing at any time in the session; and
• provided a method of working which was true to the process of IT-INSET - the pattern of preparation and planning, teaching and observing, evaluation and reflection, and further planning and preparation became firmly rooted from the first week.

We spent insufficient time clarifying and stating our brief. We may not, at this stage, have had a common understanding of what we were focusing on, except that it was to be the children's learning. In retrospect, it would have been easier for us, over the first two weeks, to make general inferences about children's spelling than to focus on spelling strategies, so a broader 'Looking at children's spelling' might have been better than 'Looking at the strategies used by children to improve their spelling.'

Throughout the six weeks, I went through much personal questioning about the role of the tutor. This should have been discussed more fully with the team. The main problem was whether or when to nudge, push, or redirect discussions. I accepted that, at first, my role would be that of facilitator and scene-setter. Anything more would have meant a prescriptive role which would be uncomfortable and contradict IT-INSET principles.

Week 2: Tuesday 16 February

Planning and preparation No preparation was necessary. The children were to self-correct the previous week's work. From this the team hoped to see different strategies in action. During the planning half hour, it was decided to regroup the children. Half the class would correct their work by themselves while the other half would work in pairs. Two students took on teaching roles and the rest of the team observed. All the team would give assistance if asked but not suggest any particular strategy.

Activity The children were given forty minutes to correct the passage and it was then re-dictated. Both the corrected sheets and the re-dictated passages were collected in.

Evaluation The team discussion was at first anecdotal, but some inferences and comments were made about the children's learning. Problems were noted in relation to how children used dictionaries (a strategy used by nearly all of them).

• Many had difficulty in finding a word when there was doubt about what made the first vowel sound.
• Many did not check the dictionary definition (e.g. when looking for 'bored' - not in the dictionary, but 'bore' was - some children were satisfied with 'board').

Many of the second pieces of dictation showed an improvement. There were no discernible differences between children working in pairs or individually (probably because those supposed to be working by themselves had discussed their work with others).

The discussion moved on to consider the difference between strategies which help a child to spell a new word and those that help to learn the spelling of a new word. We agreed that these were two distinct processes.

The following points were raised.

- Developing dictionary skills without emphasising how to learn the new word was only a short-term strategy. *(Teacher)*
- Two children working together could lead to one dominating the other so that one does not develop skills but relies on someone else. *(Student)*
- Is the team looking at what strategies children use to improve their spelling or testing to find out which are the best ones? *(Tutor and student)*
- How can the team find out what is going through their minds in order to help them? *(Student)*

Planning For the next session it was decided to look at different ways of presenting spelling. One was to encourage the children to recognise that one sound could be made by many different vowel combinations. Four digraphs (or, aw, au and ou) were chosen. These would be presented to the children in different ways and four members of the group (three students and the tutor) undertook the task of preparing an activity.

Further reflections on Week 2

Observation skills cannot be learned overnight. They need to be practised and refined. From Week 2 onwards we discussed exactly what we were trying to achieve by setting a particular piece of work. This helped us to focus our observations on the specific, although general observations were also made. Methods of observing varied, though none of us carried out structured observations using predetermined categories. We tended to concentrate on small groups (from two to six children), noting down what each child was doing at regular intervals (usually every two minutes). As a team, we needed to be better prepared for this. Watching a series of short video clips, recording what we saw, and analysing it together would have been beneficial.

We did encounter some problems in making sense of observations. At first there was little formal categorisation although we did look for patterns. We were able to refer to our notes of the problems children have in using dictionaries. We had all observed and recorded common problems which featured in further planning and evaluation sessions.

During the six weeks, all of us shared the roles of chairperson, minute taker, teacher and observer. We made the mistake of occasionally drifting between one role and another. This was particularly true when we agreed that, although observing, a team member would offer help to children when approached. Taking time out to help a child left gaps in our observation schedules. We should have made it more clear to the children whom to approach during a session.

Looking back on the evaluation notes, an opportunity may have been missed in not developing the discussion with full reference to the 'six questions' (see p. 5). We had discussed the question 'What did the pupils actually do?', and answers to 'What were they learning?' and 'How worthwhile was it?' were implicit in the free-ranging discussion. Should there have been an opportunity for us to take them on board more fully? I return to this point in Week 3.

Week 3: Tuesday 23 February

Planning and preparation Four activities had been prepared using the agreed sounds and words. There were two games, one using dice and the other a variation on 'Kim's game'. One work sheet used cloze procedure and the other presented the sounds using word games, rhymes and a crossword. The class was divided into three groups: two groups of four playing the games and the rest working on the sheets.

Activity Two students conducted the game groups. A third took charge of the class. The rest of the team concentrated on each observing a small group of children. During the session, two groups of children were tape-recorded, discussing how they approached spelling.

Evaluation The team was very pleased with the children's involvement in the activities and expressed regret that the groups had not participated in more than one of them. The following two points were made from observations, which members of the team all confirmed to some degree.

31

- The children showed real interest in the words themselves - they were looking very closely at them and seemed to be developing an appreciation of them.
- The team now appeared to be developing in-built correction so that the children naturally correct their work as they go through it.

During the session, one student and the tutor talked with eight children about their views on spelling. They talked freely about a whole range of topics linked directly or indirectly with spelling and agreed the following.

- Good spelling was very necessary (*Student:* 'Why?').
- It was important because 'It would help us pass exams'.
- It makes your work 'look good'.
- It helps you 'work quicker'.
- It helps you understand what someone has written (although one girl said she could read her friend's work even though her friend recognised she was a 'useless speller').

The conversation moved on to 'How do you know a word is spelled correctly?' At first the children gave intuitive answers such as 'Well, we just know', but it gradually became obvious that they could articulate a whole number of strategies, for example:

- by looking at the sounds within a word;
- by using a dictionary to check; or
- by changing letters around.

Some intimated that they used these hierarchically: if their first strategy failed, they would move on to the next best one.

In the team discussion, there was some measure of surprise at how well the children were able to articulate their own learning. The strategies described by the children were each checked to see if the team had evidence of their use in practice: nine of the ten strategies described had been observed.

Planning The children's apparent involvement in the activities led to a suggestion that they could perhaps make their own games. This would:

- increase their involvement with the spellings;
- let them have control over how they learned their spellings;

- involve creativity;
- allow a practical activity where recording work was not important; and
- give a different context for correct spelling.

This was prepared as the following week's activity.

Further reflections on Week 3

This week seemed to mark a critical point in the process. The level of our discussion, the inferences made from observation, our realisation that the children could articulate their own strategies, and our tentative moves towards hypothesising showed how far, and how quickly, we had moved on.

In many ways, the structure we had given to our work, even how we had allocated out time, had directed our thought. We became used to questioning our own comments and assumptions. Over the weeks, I had noted questions that had been asked by team members:

> What did we see?
> Did anyone else see that?
> Do you have any further impressions?
> Anything else to share with the group?
> How did it go?
> Why do we say that?
> What could we have done?
> How do we know they're learning?
> What does this tell us?
> Do we agree?
> Do we need to take this into account?
> Does it help us forward?
> How do we plan next week?
> What lessons have we learned so far?
> What do we want to learn?

Many of these could be related to the 'six questions' (p. 5). At the time, I remember being anxious to address the six questions directly. This was probably because it was difficult not to assume that others would place as much stock as I did on six such simple but searching questions. The other team members had not, like me, had the opportunity to internalise them but had adopted similar ways of thinking. I can only surmise that the method of working in IT-INSET encourages an analytical way of thinking about children's learning. The team had internalised this process.

Week 4: Tuesday 1 March

Planning and preparation The children had been given a printed sheet, prepared by the team the previous week, which contained suggestions for games and a list of vowel digraphs to choose from. They had several days to gather together any materials they might need. The only limitation put on them was that they should work in groups of no more than four. They could work individually if they wished.

Activity Further explanations about the activity were given by the class teacher. When the activity began, there was little pupil-teacher contact, so the whole team was involved in observation. Two groups making games were tape-recorded. At the end of the session most games were unfinished and the class teacher allocated further time during the week for their completion.

Evaluation A wide range of games was produced. All the children had to make their own lists of words and this was done in a variety of ways. Some referred back to previous exercises in their workbooks and others used their spelling texts. Those who tried to use dictionaries quickly discovered that their usefulness in this context was limited. Others went meticulously through their reading books. In the discussion of observations, the following points were made.

- There was a high level of involvement with the sounds.
- The children learned more about the sounds in the preparation of the games (choosing their own lists of words with a common sound and writing definitions or questions about them) than they would in playing the games.
- The children were using many of the strategies that they had articulated the previous week.
- The children's awareness of spelling had been heightened because they knew that this was the focus of both their work and the team's.

Further reflections on Week 4

As this week marked the half-way point of the project, the team agreed to evaluate IT-INSET as it had been experienced so far. The team questionnaire (Appendix 5) was used for this purpose. It was filled in first by individuals, and then by the team as a whole. The evaluation covered four main areas: planning, teaching/observing, discussion, and teamwork. The following were a few of the key points which arose.

Planning The topic was determined exclusively by the two class teachers. On no occasion was any member of the team left to plan or prepare for the whole class. Everyone did, however, prepare at least one activity which was used by a group of children. The team as a whole planned what to observe and discuss.

Teaching/observing All members of the team took on a teaching role at some stage. During individual completion of the questionnaire, five team members said they did not use structured observation. It emerged that they had assumed that 'structured' implied manufactured or printed check-lists. In discussing the team response, we agreed that we had all used some form of structured observation, in the sense of observation which was systematic, deliberate and focused.

Discussion After four weeks it was difficult for us to decide what was the major focus during discussions. In individual completion of the questionnaire, students and teachers said they had addressed all of the five areas identified equally - what pupils did, what pupils learned, what teachers did, what we learned, and worthwhileness. My notes, however, suggested that discussions were weighted towards what the children did. During team completion of the questionnaire, we talked at length about whether or not we had discussed what the teacher did. We agreed that we had planned what the role of the teacher would be and who should take it on, but not how they would carry it out. Nor had we evaluated the teacher's role.

After my own doubts about how we were using the 'six questions', it was reassuring to find that individual responses to the questionnaire indicated that the team considered that they had been addressing them, even if indirectly. I feel that more direct engagement with them would have sharpened our thinking.

Teamwork The team worked exceptionally well together. I noted three comments from students at the end of the first week:

> That was fun.
> You really get to find out what the children are doing.
> This is going to be worthwhile for the children and us.

This set the tone for the following weeks. There was always a sense of enthusiasm, hard work and enjoyment. Group and individual responses to the questionnaire bore out how effectively the group worked together.

The team's joint perception of roles was that the class teacher determined the topic and made things run smoothly. The college tutor organised the discussion, while the team planned classroom work and shared in running things smoothly.

Week 5: Tuesday 8 March

Planning and preparation The children were to play their own and others' games. Only a little time was spent in planning. Most of the half hour was spent in discussing what evidence the team might try to collect through observation. One of the students suggested that observation in pairs would perhaps allow different interpretations of the same observations and lead to more discussion. This method was accepted by the team. The whole team admitted that they had found it difficult to make inferences or draw out evidence from the observations made.

Activity The children played their games for the first time. During the week, they had written out the rules and made lists of the words they were using. Each individual or group had also prepared tests to try to see if, by playing the game, their spelling improved. This idea came from one of the groups and was not teacher initiated. The children played with obvious enjoyment. Each group played at least two games and all the class expressed a desire to play all of the games.

Evaluation The first twenty minutes were spent discussing the games. Although many needed to be refined and to have clearer instructions, both teachers felt that the children had produced material which would become a valuable permanent resource. Only a slight improvement was noted in the tests the children carried out before and after playing the games. This was probably because the children had already become familar with the words during the preparation of the games.

The chairperson, a student, directed the team to the questions which had been posed before the activity:

What had the team seen?
What could be made of it?

So far as the first question was concerned, the team had made copious notes of their observations. In relation to the second, one teacher pointed out that hypotheses based on observation had been used and these had guided planning. The team recalled hypotheses of this kind that had been used.

- Self-correction should be encouraged as a way to improve spelling.
- Poor pronunciation can hinder good spelling.
- Children need to be encouraged to read through their work when they have finished and reading aloud helps to identify mistakes.
- Children need to be actively involved with words in a variety of ways.
- Correcting in pairs can be beneficial.
- There needs to be a positive, progressive approach to dictionary skills.
- Teachers need to be aware when to intervene when a child has a problem - early intervention may solve a problem but may not help the learning of a skill.
- Children should be encouraged to think about and articulate their own spelling strategies.

Planning The final week's activity would again involve a dictated passage which the children would then self-correct. When they have finished this, they will be able to continue playing their spelling games or work from a prepared sheet.

Further reflections on Week 5

It was becoming obvious that we were now engaging in applying theory based on our analysis of practice. We were also both evaluating and developing this area of the curriculum. What is interesting is how we reached this stage.

On more than one occasion, we had discussed the fact that all of us - teachers, tutor, students and children - were involved in a learning process. We were moving forward together, though at different rates and from different starting points. As we observed the children developing their own skills, we were prompted to refine, adapt, and even revise previous statements that we had made.

I had posed the questions:

What had we learned?
What do we do next?
Have we developed any theories about spelling?

At first, responses were slow to come. One student enthused that not only had she learned just how complex spelling was, but also she had gained a collection of strategies that she could use in future. Another noted how different approaches had benefited different children and how rigidly sticking to one approach meant that certain children would miss out. Perhaps this would be obvious to the established teacher, but coming to this realisation from practical experience was far more relevant than notes taken in the lecture theatre.

It was one of the teachers who insisted that we had been actively theorising. Although many of our statements might seem to be stating the obvious, he felt that they gained new clarity by their articulation and could be better appreciated for use in future planning. The time that had been set aside for reflection had given both teachers the opportunity to think about what was normally routine. Without such time for reflection, any thought about the last activity was lost in the preparation for the next. It was the difficulty of finding this time outside an IT-INSET programme that would hinder, though not prevent, future reflection.

A short, but very interesting discussion followed on the difference between hypothesising and theorising. The team agreed that we were hypothesising because we were treating a statement as something that was tentative which would guide our planning but not dictate our future actions. We were not researchers looking for a definitive statement. We were responding to a situation and adapting and redefining our approach.

Within the team, there was confidence to hypothesise. I asked directly how we had got to this stage. It became clear that the team felt it was less important what questions one asked oneself than that one was questioning in the first place. Perhaps we should have reviewed in more detail how our thinking had developed.

Week 6: Tuesday 8 March

Planning and preparation The extract to be read had been chosen the previous week. It was the picnic scene from *The Iron Man* by Ted Hughes. The criterion for selection was that it contained many of the sounds we had covered over the five weeks. One of the teachers had made a tape-recording of the extract. Six sets of headphones were set up in one of the quiet rooms so that the children could use this throughout the session. The class was split into two for the reading of the dictation passage. A sheet containing word games and rhymes had been prepared for when they had finished their work.

Activity As planned.

Evaluation The team had agreed that this session would be in two parts - an evaluation of the activity, and an evaluation of IT-INSET as the team had experienced it. Both parts were to be recorded and used as a basis for a report to the school staff.

The following brief extract from the recording gives a flavour of the evaluation of the activity.

> *Tutor:* Today, Amisha was looking for 'munching' but it wasn't in the dictionary. She spent so long ...
> *Teacher 1:* Did she find 'munch'? Brendan found 'munch' and made the connection.
> *Student 1:* One of them found 'munch' and added 'ing' to that.
> *Student 2:* Sonal and Rakhee were working together. They were comparing each other's work and looking for words that didn't match. Then they'd have a chat and go to a dictionary to find out which word was right or if both of them were wrong.
> *Tutor:* Certainly that's a strategy that has come out of the type of work we've been doing. They wouldn't have done that before.
> *Teacher 2:* Getting back to what we did in the first week. Did anyone see or hear them reading their work aloud, either to themselves or to someone else? *(Sounds of confirmation.)*

Student 3: Yes, Bhavin was reading it, and reading it out how it was actually spelt. It was really good. You could see him sounding it out and realising that he had made a mistake.

Teacher 2: That's right, because I marked his and the mistakes that he was making were like putting 'bolw' for 'bowl'. You can see that, reading it out carefully, looking at each letter, he realised the mistake and corrected it. So perhaps we could look at some kind of rank order of self-correction of spellings for children. First of all, maybe, the reading of it out loud and then to each other, then looking at a dictionary, then going to the teacher for advice if they can't find it. These children seem to know these and other strategies now. You see, for many children, looking at a dictionary isn't immediately the best answer for them.

Student 2: I was talking to Rakhee and Sonal about the words they had to look up in the dictionary and they said that in order to remember the spelling they picture the bit they got wrong. Then they picture the correction. They explained it with a word that had a missing 'e'.

Tutor: Sukhninder and Amisha actually went through all the 'o' sounds. I wasn't exactly sure what they were doing, so I talked to them about it. They were thinking about the various combinations to make 'roasted'. They were going through 'oa', 'ow', 'ou', and 'o' and then some that they discarded because they realised immediately it was the wrong sound. If we're talking about a hierarchy of skills then that is really very sophisticated.

Teacher 2: I used the tape-recorder with one group [playing the dictated piece again] and the concentration was truly amazing. You could almost feel it. Forget about the spelling - there's also the listening. Just getting them to concentrate and listen. Not only were they listening to the sounds in the words, but they were getting the construction of the sentence.

In the second part of the session - evaluating the IT-INSET experience - we focused our discussion around a number of questions. With regard to the key question 'What had the children learned?' we believed, from our observation, taped conversation and inference, that the children had learned:

• a self-correction plan, based on the strategies mentioned in Week 3 - this was apparently being used outside the IT-INSET sessions;

- how to focus on a topic and become involved;
- that spelling could be fun;
- that teachers do not expect a perfect copy first time - most written work benefits from correction and redrafting; and
- how to work as a team in making and playing games.

Our answers to the other questions can be illustrated by further verbatim extracts from the discussion.

What did we, as individuals, get out of it?

> *Student 2: (Laughing)* The Blockbuster game that the children made [to use on my next teaching practice].
> *Teacher 1:* I think, honestly, as the class teacher, the chance to observe the class. It's good to be able to stand back and look at a group and see the work they're doing. Whether or not it's work that you set. It's looking at what they're doing and how they're doing it.
> *Tutor:* This is an unusual situation. Eight adults in one class. But allowing for that, is observation and then evaluation based on evidence collected feasible on a day-to-day basis?
> *Teacher 1:* It probably would be and certainly would be useful. There's no problem if you structure the work ...
> *Student 4:* ... they all tend to get on so well and know what to do.
> *Teacher 1:* But it would vary from class to class.
> *Student 2:* There'd be too much for us to think about at first [as probationary teachers].
> *Teacher 2:* But if you don't, then you'll miss many of the problems that might exist in the class.
> *Student 2:* At first I could see myself evaluating in a less formal manner than specifically sitting, taking notes and then trying to sort something out from them.
> *Student 4:* In my first class [on teaching practice] you didn't have a minute to yourself to catch breath, let alone see what was going on, whereas in this class I knew I could quite easily, even as a student talking to them, take out a minute to see what was happening. I don't know about younger children though.
> *Teacher 2:* Even with younger ones, it's a good idea - even more necessary to engineer it. There are ways of engineering sessions - colouring, free choice in groups - to make yourself

available to see what one group is actually doing.

Tutor: We do it all the time if the head or a colleague comes in. Then we're able to find two minutes.

Student 1: It's made me just more aware. The way we've focused in on spelling and the way we've used games. Before, I don't think I could have seen the value. It wasn't the playing of them to learn the spellings but what went into the making of them.

Student 4: It was really interesting talking to the children about spelling. We'd say that you need to spell so that you can understand each other, but the children said they could understand it even though the spellings weren't right. Really, we're thinking just in an adult world. We've got to be aware of that.

How did we analyse practice, apply theory or hypothesise?

Teacher 2: We didn't look at what was happening before we started. We didn't see how far we taught them and what strategies were being used six weeks ago.

Student 4: We didn't analyse practice from the baseline.

Student 3: Did we use hypotheses?

Student 5: Of course we did.

Student 2: We set out to find what strategies they used. The hypothesis was that children had strategies. We tried to find out what they were and how they used them.

Teacher 2: We also theorised that reading aloud would help children realise where they had made a mistake, also that sometimes teaching children similar sounds together would help them in learning which one to use.

How far did we develop the curriculum?

Teacher 1: We really did make the children aware of different strategies. The children seemed to be using these strategies in all their written work.

Teacher 2: It's meant building self-correction into the curriculum. This is something we've talked about as a staff but we've made it more obvious. You've got to hammer it, that so much correction can come from the children rather than elsewhere. Instead of taking a book home, marking it and then the child writing out the words again, if children are an integral part of the correction and marking process, then they are more likely to remember the spelling.

Presenting the IT-INSET experience

As the best way of involving others in the IT-INSET process, the team decided to make a presentation to the rest of the staff of the school. The whole team met together for about three hours at the local teachers' centre to prepare and plan the presentation.

I had written a report based on our last team discussion, when we had been evaluating the experience, and the first part of the team meeting was spent discussing this. Both teachers felt the staff should all have copies before the presentation and they undertook the task of duplicating and circulating it.

The following agenda was agreed for the presentation:

1. Introduction of team *(Headteacher)*
2. The background to IT-INSET *(Tutor)*
3. How IT-INSET worked at the school *(Student 2)*
4. The school view of IT-INSET *(Student 4)*
5. The teacher view of IT-INSET *(Teacher 1)*
6. What did we learn? *(Teacher 2)*
7. An open discussion relating IT-INSET work to the school language policy and implications for the future *(Team)*

While the teachers and two students discussed how they would present their views of IT-INSET, the rest of the team began work on a display. This involved the use of photographs taken during the six weeks, examples of children's work, and information about IT-INSET. The students and tutor agreed to meet two hours before the presentation to put up the display in the school hall.

All eighteen of the school staff were present on 21 April, although the Headteacher sent his apologies, having been called to a liaison meeting with the local high school.

The two students who were to speak were obviously nervous as the presentation began, but the way in which they expressed themselves and coped with the pressure of speaking in front of so many teachers was commendable. One spoke of the boost in confidence it had given her to work so closely alongside experienced teachers and how her thoughts about one area of the curriculum had developed through the process of IT-INSET.

She also spoke about how the IT-INSET approach could be adapted to everyday teaching. This prompted two of the school staff to suggest that IT-INSET appeared artificial, as it relied on eight adults being in a teaching area. They felt that what the children had achieved in this situation was both unfair on the teacher for the future and unreal in the normal school context. I suggested that the whole team would agree that if we had been concerned solely about children producing something at the end of six weeks (games, stories, or whatever) what we had done would be artificial. But the benefits of IT-INSET were in developing particular ways of seeing the complexities of the classroom and reviewing the curriculum. This would benefit the children in the future.

The two teacher members of the team commented on the problems of observing one's own class without the benefit of the team's presence, but said they believed it was possible. One member of staff wanted to know if the project had altered the way in which the class teacher taught. He said his teaching would be affected, not only by what he had learned about spelling, but by how he had learned it. Another member of staff who had previously worked in an IT-INSET team at the school said the experience had had an effect on her teaching, but the problem was maintaining the impetus when the team had disbanded.

Following the presentation, there was an informal discussion which lasted for 45 minutes. A major point raised was that, while the staff appreciated and valued this meeting, they felt they should have been made more aware of what was happening at the beginning of the IT-INSET programme. Some confessed to having no knowledge at all of what had been happening in the school. Nevertheless, at the end of the session there was majority agreement that both the outcomes and the method of working had direct relevance to curriculum review in general and, more specifically, to the current review of language policy within the school.

3

Seaton Junior School

Gerald Sewell, on whose report (Sewell 1987) this case study is based, was one of the eight teacher-members of an IT-INSET team which also included eight students, two tutors and six parent governors. It illustrates an elaboration of the IT-INSET pattern in involving all of the staff of a primary school and all of the children. As Deputy Headteacher, Gerald Sewell reflects a distinctively school view of IT-INSET. He began with clear aspirations for the possible contribution of such an undertaking to the curriculum development and changes in attitudes and practice for which he believed his school was ready. This chapter recounts the effects of IT-INSET and analyses the particular qualities of the process which seemed to achieve them.

Seaton Junior School is a voluntary-controlled Church of England school serving the village of Seaton (population 5,000) in West Cumbria. The well-equipped school buildings were opened in 1974, and consist of a hall and two large open-plan areas, each accommodating four classes. The roll is rising slightly, with 225 children aged between 7 and 11. There are eight teachers, in addition to the Head.

In the Autumn Term of 1986, the Headteacher and his Deputy welcomed the opportunity of engaging in IT-INSET with Charlotte Mason College, Ambleside. In discussions between the school and College, the purposes of the programme were defined as:

• to provide an opportunity for the whole staff of the school to work together in the development of the mathematics curriculum;
• to allow college students, college tutors and school governors to

share in, and contribute to, this curriculum development; and
• to enable practising teachers, students in initial training and training institution tutors to develop professionally through co-operative work as equal partners.

The IT-INSET team consisted of all eight teachers at Seaton Junior School and the Head, eight third-year students (all mathematics specialists), and two college tutors. Unusually, six school governors (all parents) were also full members of the team. The focus of the team's work was a problem-solving approach to mathematics, taking as a starting point the section of Cumbria Education Committee's *Mathematics 5-11* (1986) on problem solving and investigations. The aim was to develop a progression in problem solving throughout the four years of the junior school, including consideration of:

• choice of appropriate problems, or kinds of problems, for each year group;
• problem-solving strategies and possible progression in their development;
• the school's existing scheme of work in mathematics, in order to make decisions about what could be omitted to make space to accomodate problem solving.

Organisation of IT-INSET

The project took place over twelve full days in the Autumn Term, which were allocated as shown in Figure 3.1. Seven of these days were used in planning and discussion meetings of various kinds. The other five were project days when the mornings were devoted to activities with the children and the afternoons to discussion. For the first half-hour of a project day, the Headteacher or his Deputy took a whole school assembly, enabling the rest of the team to meet to finalise their planning of the day. For the remaining two hours of the morning, a teacher and student worked together in each class, with the two tutors and the Headteacher joining these mini-teams as appropriate.

During these periods, problem-solving activities were tried out in the various classes either with small groups of children or with the whole class (and occasionally with the two classes of a year-group together or with the whole of the upper or lower half of the school).

Figure 3.2 is an example of one of the activities tried out in the fourth year.

Figure 3.1   The IT-INSET calendar at Seaton

---

23 September	Students and tutors meet at College
27 September	Full team meet at College
30 September	Students and tutors meet at College
7 October	Full team meeting day at school
14 October	Project day 1
21 October	Project day 2
28 October	Students and tutors meet at College
4 November	Full team meeting day at school
11 November	Project day 3
18 November	Project day 4
25 November	Project day 5
2 December	Full team meeting day at school

Figure 3.2   A fourth-year problem-solving activity

Equal steps

(a)	2	☐ ☐ ☐	14
(b)	7	☐ ☐ ☐	39
(c)	10	☐ ☐ ☐	58
(d)	8	☐ ☐ ☐	52
(e)	15	☐ ☐ ☐	63
(f)	9	☐ ☐ ☐	39

Are any impossible?
Can you show how you know they are possible or impossible?
Can you think of other examples of possible and impossible?
Can you find a rule?
Make a poster.

Sometimes a student initiated an activity, sometimes a teacher, and sometimes a teacher and student worked together. Teachers, students and tutors all had opportunities for observing others in action and for joining in activities other than the ones they had initiated. Governors acted as observers, making notes about how a group of children tackled an activity, or asking a group appropriate questions. The distinction between initiators, participants and observers became blurred for most of the time, and some difficulties were experienced in stepping quickly from one role into another.

For the first half of the afternoon of each project day, three supply teachers were available to take three of the classes. Seaton teachers took three other classes and pairs of students the remaining two, leaving the other five teachers and four students to meet the two tutors and the Headteacher in two groups to discuss the morning's work and to plan the next project day. For the second half of the afternoon the other four students and three other teachers taught classes, leaving the rest of the team free for further discussion and planning meetings.

Supply cover was also made available by Cumbria Education Authority on days when there were planning meetings of the whole team either at the College or in school - a total of eighteen supply teacher days for the whole project. In addition, the school staff met regularly at the end of the school day.

The views of the Deputy Headteacher

At the end of the Autumn Term, the Deputy Headteacher reported on the project in the following terms (adapted from Sewell 1987).

There is nothing new about a workshop approach to INSET, but in this venture, because of the involvement of the College, the resources on which we could draw were considerably greater than they would otherwise have been. With eight full-time teachers plus the Headteacher, eight third-year students and their two tutors, and an allowance for supply cover when class teachers were involved in meetings, it was possible to put into effect what I would call the ideal model for a school-based workshop. The area on which we chose to focus our attention was the problem-solving/ investigational approach to mathematics teaching.

In meetings after school and in the periods made available through the use of supply cover, we were able to plan the activities we intended to introduce in the working sessions. In some instances, meeting just as a school staff, we could exchange ideas in a very informal way and this was particularly helpful to one or two individuals who showed some signs of nervousness in the early stages. When we met with the students and their tutors, either as a whole team or as members of sub-groups, the initial 'us and them' barrier very quickly disappeared.

The opportunity for teachers, students and tutors to talk informally during the classroom working sessions was an extremely important element in the success of the project. After the activity had been initiated, members of the team could work with the children and talk with their colleagues at the same time. My own opinion is that it is this talk, or rather the changing quality of this talk, which holds the key to the broadening of experience and the expansion of awareness.

Having taken part in a shared experience, it was in the debriefing sessions in the afternoons of the project days that the most useful discussions took place. The opportunity to talk about the shared experience helped feelings of reserve to evaporate. The governors who were involved in the project took part in all the discussions. They became markedly more enthusiastic and relaxed as the project progressed and certainly learned just as much as the rest of us.

It is difficult to describe the increasing measure of openness and absence of self-consciousness which manifested itself. It affected everyone - the children in a number of subtle ways, the students, the tutors, the governors and the Seaton teachers alike. In the discussion groups, even those individuals who had at first been very reticent talked more freely about the successes and failures of the activities which had been tried out in the working sessions. It became abundantly clear that, as the programme wore on, a number of changes were taking place in the way in which teachers (and almost certainly the students also) saw the whole programme, their place within it, and their perception of the nature of the problem-solving approach to mathematics teaching.

Everyone, including the children, got something out of the whole exercise and, as one would expect, the extent to which they did so depended almost entirely on the effort which they put into it. If we can walk away from an event with the knowledge that we now see something differently, then we can say we have learned something in an enabling situation. That is what this project provided - an enabling situation for both teachers and children.

While the children were learning mathematics through problem solving and the investigational approach, the school staff were learning about alternative teaching strategies and the quality of different learning experiences, and thus developing their own awareness as professionals. It is perhaps surprising how much of a major shift in our ways of thinking seems to be necessary to realise that the needs of children as learners and the needs of teachers as learners can be satisfied at one and the same time and, most importantly, that this can be done without reducing the importance of either. In fact, the reverse is the case - when we recognise the needs of both groups of learners and set up an enabling situation for both pupils and teachers, the quality of the learning experiences for both groups can be enhanced.

I am in no doubt that our model worked and that the enabling situation was effective, though it affected individuals in different ways and to different extents. As any observer would be able to confirm, the children enjoyed the work and were certainly engaged in productive learning. In the words of the governors' report on the project:

> The most important fact to us is that the children enjoyed it. It did not always follow that the more able children coped best. Less able children, and in fact *all* children, had more confidence to ask if they did not understand. When we asked the children the questions, 'What are you doing? How? Why?' they were able to answer positively. The fact that they were enjoying the work meant they were learning from it. As parents we have had the feedback, 'Oh, it's Tuesday - good!' not, 'Oh, it's Tuesday. Oh no, not maths all day.'

The quality of the activities was generally high and some were first rate. As members of the team became more confident in their own abilities, the teaching strategies involved became markedly more appropriate, with some near-perfect intervention strategies being used by teachers and students alike. There is no doubt that we all learned from one another. We learned a lot from the students; I am sure they learned something from us. Most of all, we learned from the children. Once teachers break away from the hang-up of feeling that they are assumed to be expert in everything, and that therefore it is somehow wrong for them to be seen to be learning, enormous leaps can be made.

There have been, and probably always will be, difficulties in bringing teachers to a full realisation of the need for an investigational approach to teaching. Though lip service is paid to the notion that children can learn mathematics through problem solving at different levels, and open hostility to this approach may not be much in evidence, the same old defensive stances still emerge. The 'whole school workshop' approach which we adopted certainly facilitated change. It seems to me to be quite obvious that if teachers are to develop their professional awareness and gain more insight into the teaching/learning process then the proper place to do this is in their own schools, with children and colleagues whom they know, and in a familiar setting. Teacher learning cannot occur in a place where there is no opportunity to observe and experience children learning also.

In addition to the school-based context for the work, a number of factors contributed to the success of the programme.

• The built-in provision for supply cover, enabling meetings to take place during the school day, was critical.
• The presence of students was vital in a number of ways. The freshness and enthusiasm which they brought was one important ingredient, but they also brought a great deal in the way of ideas and resources. They were treated as colleagues of equal standing to ourselves.
• The presence of extra adults was also important. They were not used simply to reduce the size of the teaching groups. Their value lay chiefly in the fact that it was possible to arrange matters so that we could observe each other working, and discussion could take place while we were working with children.

Initial and in-service teacher education have been organised in many different ways, but only rarely at one and the same time. The provision of INSET, in particular, is undergoing important changes at the present time and it is our view at Seaton that the model which we used in the Autumn Term of 1986 should be looked at closely with a view to wider application. Although the effectiveness of the programme in the longer term still has to be judged, we are clear that, as it worked at the time, it could hardly have been improved upon. In terms of what children, teachers, governors, students and tutors got out of the programme, it was certainly a success. In terms of ecomomy of expenditure, it is difficult to imagine anything of a similar cost reaching and affecting so many individuals, all of whom learned something of importance and found it hard work and immensely enjoyable.

No other model for INSET that I have so far encountered has been so peculiarly effective as this. The 'visiting expert' model, working with perhaps one teacher at a time, is certainly not as effective. Neither is the model of 'sending someone off on a course', hoping that when they return they will be able to communicate what they have learned to the rest of the staff. If change is to take place, if we truly want to learn, we have to work at it together as a staff.

Our future plans, at least in broad outline and intention, are already laid. They were made in recognition that we live in the real world. They are therefore modest and intentionally simple. What would be most useful to us would be the certainty that at some future date we could again draw upon the resources of Charlotte Mason College. It is certainly possible that, after an initial input of IT-INSET, a school might be quite capable of continuing a policy of staff and curriculum development. I would visualise, however, that at some stage it would be necessary to arrange for a 'booster injection'. I can see no reason why this should not be a similarly organised IT-INSET programme.

Over the next year, we have the following intentions.

1. To arrange for three project days per term. The model used throughout the IT-INSET programme will be applied as far as possible, with some modifications. We may work as lower-school and upper-school units rather than as a whole school. At this stage it is our intention to focus on investigative mathematics teaching.
2. To develop a more investigative approach to mathematics teaching in individual classes and teaching areas.
3. To encourage a team-teaching approach, in classes of the same year groups, to become a more regular feature of the timetable.
4. To develop a more reflective attitude generally towards our own practices through the keeping of field notebooks.
5. To attempt to extend these ways of working to other curriculum areas. Language development and science may be obvious choices.

These are, I hope, the correct and logical steps which we ought to take as a school. If we do not achieve our objectives, I am clear in my own mind that the reasons will not be found in any flaw in the design of the initial IT-INSET programme. As I hope the above account shows, the programme has had a very significant impact on Seaton Junior School. The quality of the experience was of the highest order, and this has been recognised by all of the teachers who took part in it.

Postscript

Fifteen months later, it was possible to report that most of these intentions had been realised.

1. Three project days per term proved unattainable, but two half-day sessions as a follow-up to the IT-INSET work on problem solving in mathematics were organised in the remainder of the 1986/87 school year. In the first of these, the Acting Headteacher took the four classes of the lower half of the school for a morning to free the four lower-school teachers to work with their four upper-school colleagues. (The Deputy was Acting Headteacher during the calendar year 1987 while the Headteacher was taking part in a Commonwealth exchange.) The brief for the lower-school teachers was:

• to prepare three activities for upper juniors and try them out; and
• to help and observe their opposite numbers in the upper school.

In the second half-day, this arrangement was reversed, with the four upper-school teachers being freed to work with their lower-school colleagues. In the words of the Headteacher, these half-day sessions were designed to emphasise that 'progression and continuity are the main thrust of our curriculum development in mathematics.'

2. The Headteacher believes that the IT-INSET project has had a significant effect in raising awareness of the investigational approach, and that 'all the staff now understand what we're trying to do.' He adds, 'I see evidence around the school of people being prepared to have a go.' A senior adviser visiting the school observed, 'These kids have been brought up on problem solving.' The Headteacher comments, 'They haven't, but this indicates the progress we have made with the problem-solving approach.'

3. The Headteacher recognises that many teachers find Seaton Junior is a difficult school to work in because of its open-plan layout. In a sense the choice of mathematics as the subject area for the Autumn Term project was subsidiary to the expected effect of stimulating teachers to work together in teams. The Headteacher and his Deputy share the view that many of the staff now see more clearly the advantages of working in teams and are working together more both

as a staffroom team and as classroom teams as a result of the IT-INSET project. Progress is intermittent, however, often because of outside pressures such as staff changes, secondments, and sickness.

4. Many staff are now making good use of field notebooks. These are intended for teachers to jot down bright ideas, snatches of classroom conversation, observations made during teaching, etc. Particular use has been made of them during the follow-up mathematics project days and the science IT-INSET days. A brief example from one teacher's field notebook will perhaps serve as an illustration (Figure 3.3).

Figure 3.3   Extract from a field notebook

Science, 5 March 1987
Shapes in nature and building
Practical lesson of designing shapes and colouring. Then children encouraged to discuss their patterns. Practical successful but oral discussion limited in standard as children have poor listening and discussion skills.
Follow-up action: Emphasise listening to others' opinions and points of view. Silence when someone else 'has the floor'. Turns at expressing point of view. The value of each other's opinion.

---

5. In the Autumn Term of 1987, a further IT-INSET project was engaged in with Charlotte Mason College. The focus this time was on integrating science into the curriculum, as well as on encouraging the upper-school staff to work as a team. The project was on a somewhat smaller scale than the one the year before, involving the four upper-school teachers on eight days with six second-year students and one tutor. Supply cover was available, but it was not necessary to use as much as in the mathematics programme, since the new teacher contract was by this time in force and two school INSET days were used for meetings at the College.

More recently, at the suggestion of one teacher, the staff have begun working together on patterns of children's behaviour. The aim is for teachers to become better co-ordinated with each other and with parents in approaches to children on matters of behaviour. A list of key topics relating to behaviour has been made at an initial staff discussion meeting. As a next stage, each teacher has chosen an area in which to do some more work in order to contribute to the next stage of discussion. This is seen by the Headteacher as an important illustration of the increased openness which has followed from the school's involvement in IT-INSET and in particular from the 'whole staff workshop' approach adopted.

4

Wycliffe Community College

This case study was compiled by Richard Hickman, the tutor-member of a secondary school team, from the specially written reflections of his two teacher and five student colleagues. This is therefore a distinctively team perspective on IT-INSET. In acting as co-ordinator of the writing and as provider of a framework for it, Richard Hickman has sought to mirror his tutor role in the team throughout the programme.

Wycliffe Community College is set in a large council estate in one of the most deprived areas of Leicester. The building has recently been refurbished and provides attractive accommodation with large open-plan carpeted areas. It caters for upwards of 500 children between 11 and 16 years of age. There are some forty teachers and a particularly strong system of pastoral care.

The school has a first-year base in which the Principal, in company with the teachers concerned, aims to reflect typical primary school practice during the difficult transition into the fragmented world of a secondary school. In particular, the intentions are to develop more group work and to loosen subject boundaries so that areas of work serve several aspects of the curriculum. Staff see the children's limited communication skills as a major hindrance to effective work of this kind.

The college specifically sought an IT-INSET team of tutor and students drawn from different subject areas, so that a range of perspectives would be built into the joint planning and evaluation. The team's brief was to experiment with group work in cross-curricular topics of the teachers' choosing, paying particular attention to observing the effects on the children's listening and talking skills.

Getting started

Alan, a mathematics student, explains what getting started on IT-INSET meant to him:

> I read quite closely a document produced by our IT-INSET co-ordinator *The organisation of IT-INSET in Leicestershire* (Everton, undated). I remember reading it over lunch, my interest having been aroused that morning by the enthusiasm that I sensed projecting from the staff at the School of Education. Going out to schools in an IT-INSET team, they said, 'adds to the authenticity and value of the courses which students receive.' I read the preamble: 'Choosing the issue or focus', 'Working together', 'Team meetings', 'Written records', 'Roles', and finally 'How do the members of the team benefit?' I was impressed and I remember wondering whether it could really be that we were going to be given a real say in everything, whether we were really to experiment within the classroom. I felt very happy at least to have the opportunity. Teaching practice is very useful, but the golden rule is to adapt to common practice. The scope to be creative is limited, and rightly so to begin with for a novice teacher.
>
> In the little pamphlet I underlined the aims suggested for team meetings. They appealed again to my creative and adventurous nature: 'Describe the learning, analyse what has taken place and, drawing from both theory and practice, modify the teaching to improve pupils' learning experiences and the quality of their learning.' Nothing seems impossible to a fresh-eyed student-teacher.
>
> With this background, plus all my preconceptions, expectations and views of the nature of IT-INSET, teamwork and teaching methods, and looking forward to a taste of real democracy in school, we made our first contact with a member of the school. We were told that the team's topic had already been chosen and was under way. Reality hit me with a gentle thump. The first meeting in the IT-INSET calendar is always like this, it seems. The school must plan, so our hand is forced, the apparent freedom and flexibility restricted.
> But it soon became clear to me in the course of our team meetings that evaluating the smallest of learning experiences

is time-consuming, very intensive and open to good debate. I was relieved that our brief had been limited.

Ian, an integrated humanities student, had mixed expectations. While excited by the potential of the IT-INSET idea, he was unclear about how it might actually work, especially after the experience of his first teaching practice:

> I jumped at the chance to take part in cross-curricular work. I thrive on the unknown, the chance to try out new ideas and different ways of doing things. I was genuinely looking forward to seeing a mathematician's view of the work and the way they teach. This is fundamental to integrated humanities - teaching that encompasses lots of connected subjects, materials and media. Also, I was looking forward to the chance to experiment as fully as possible with different teaching media and techniques and having the back-up of a team. My first teaching practice had been more like survival than teaching, with no scope for development, due to the constraints of classroom management and the eternal syllabus. But I wondered how the 'proper' teachers might receive us meddling students - whether we would be taken seriously. Allied with this was a concern about having my teaching, control and management assessed and criticised. And having to perform on the spot for one lesson a week in a foreign school and then trying to tell the resident teachers what they ought to be doing seemed a ludicrous suggestion.

Debbie, a French teacher in her second year of teaching, also had reservations:

> When I was informed that I was to be part of the IT-INSET initiative I was frankly not impressed! The prospect of losing one of my precious non-contact periods, leaving me with just three - and all on a Friday - was not appealing.

This range of initial responses is not unusual. Yet nor is the fact that, at the end of the day, most participants would be prepared to be involved in IT-INSET all over again. Even Debbie:

> At the beginning of the term I had few expectations. Now I would welcome the opportunity to take part again. I feel that

the first-year team as a whole has benefited from the experience both in the way new work is planned and in the quality of learning experiences we can offer our students.

What happened to change Debbie's mind and to make the project such a valuable experience for all of us? To answer this, members of the team explain how we were able to organise learning opportunities for each other and what we learned from them. We learned by observing, by experimenting, through planning and evaluation, through a cross-curricular approach and, above all, through genuine collaboration.

Learning by observing

After four weeks of undertaking a variety of class teaching and observation roles, the team decided to teach the children in small groups. The main purpose of this was to give us an opportunity to get closer to the children's learning. Debbie explains how this arrangement helped her:

We always appointed someone to observe the sessions. I found the observations of Keith, an English as a second language student, invaluable. He had noticed that some of the team were trying to push the pupils in the direction we perceived most appropriate to their learning. I was working with a group of eight of the less able pupils who were designing a housing estate of their own. Having agreed on the need for houses, shops and a school, they decided they would also include a resident artist, a photographer and an army barracks! My suggestion of an industrial estate was greeted with indifference by the pupils, whose objective was to create *their* ideal community. Outvoted, I retired to the sidelines and observed the process by which they achieved this objective. I began to realise that imposing my own perception of a community merely served to dampen the pupils' enthusiasm by removing the control they had over their work. It became obvious that if learning is to take place then we have to start with the experiences of the pupils themselves. Firmly put in my place, I realised that my role must never be one of imparter of knowledge but rather facilitator. I had been told this during my teacher training but it took this group of pupils and the interest they were showing through taking control of their own work to remind me of its importance. They also showed me how much *all* pupils have to offer. Under normal class conditions the members of this group of pupils were the least motivated and the most self-effacing.

Ian writes of a similar experience:

The team had noticed how groups seemed to develop better if the teacher held back and acted as facilitator. I devised a simple idea of a picture of a house in a countryside setting. A group I was working with made up a story from this and eventually decided to make a play. The result, from a group of low ability, quiet girls, was a really interesting play on the school stage totally organised by them. In fact, they organised me! They controlled me as an 'extra' on the stage. It was quite frightening seeing the group's control go out of my hands, but I learned a lot from this pupils' eye view.

Learning by experimenting

Eileen is an experienced teacher in the first year base, with a responsibility for special needs. At the end of the project, she wrote:

We have been able to try out a number of strategies with smaller groups, giving us the confidence and knowledge to try them now with full classes. We have been able to let the pupils become the teachers. Without the team we would never have had a chance to do this. Having learned from the pupils, revived our early enthusiasm for trying out new strategies, and grown more confident from the experiences of the last few weeks, we have once more become pupil-oriented teachers, questioning together and trying out new strategies.

Learning through planning and evaluation

Máire, a mathematics student, was quite clear that:

The most important part of IT-INSET was discussion before and after the lessons. A large part of team meetings was spent talking over the reasons behind the work we intended to do and commenting upon previous lessons. This was useful because, although it seemed to me at times that the same things were being raised, it was only by this continuing dissection of the work that we started to notice exactly what was happening. When a lesson on teaching practice did not go as I hoped, I was left feeling as though I had failed. It was completely different during IT-INSET. When a lesson had gone awry, I could pick the brains of the other members of the team: a lesson going wrong meant more to talk and think about. The whole attitude of the team throughout the ten weeks was positive. What have we learned from this? What could we change? Why would we change something? How could we change it for the better?

If a lesson went well we talked about the reasons for this too. Were we thinking in terms of the pupils sitting quietly at their desks? Their finished products? How much teachers and pupils enjoyed the lesson, or how much writing the pupils produced?

Ian endorses the value of planning and evaluating together:

The back-up from team members was very valuable, with advice on when to step in and when to structure and direct just to keep the ball rolling. It was really important to have the appraisal that my drama was a worthwhile activity as I was beginning to wonder about its usefulness as a learning experience - especially with other groups producing dioramas or maps or videos. Sometimes when you are involved in a project you have a distorted view of the proceedings.

Learning through a cross-curricular approach

As mentioned earlier, Ian was very excited by the possibilities of a cross-curricular team:

The cross-curricular nature of the team helped to give students and teachers alike a genuine interest in seeing different curricular perspectives. This helped to give equality to team members and created a desire to participate in discussions and team policy making. There were a lot of learning situations for me and I have subsequently used many teaching methods and strategies that I saw in action then. The diversity of activities was tremendous, with small groups working all over the base area at times. One occasion saw a couple of role-play games, a diorama of a community being constructed, an annotated map being drawn of the local area, and my group making a story around a picture. A very important point was the planning of activities by individual team members in the morning with evaluation in the afternoon. This gave us all a chance to hear a method or plan talked through, perhaps to see it in action in another corner of the base, and then to analyse it. I found it very useful to hear of different methods and ideas which I could adapt without going through them myself or reading about some dry methodology which often does little to inspire me and does not give me the confidence to use it.

Learning through genuine collaboration

We would all agree that the most powerful learning experience was that of collaboration. This was fundamental to the success of the team and the enjoyment of the whole project, as Alan makes clear:

It appears that the more successful the team, the more enthusiastic and flexible the school staff have been throughout the IT-INSET work. The willingness to accept team decisions, and especially the student-teacher proposals, has proved the making of the whole project. It is equally important for student-teachers to do likewise.

The whole ethos of co-operation and shared ownership was very, very important. Working as a team, the introductory booklet says (Everton, undated), 'ALL members of the team participate in ALL aspects of the team's work:
- they PLAN the work as a team;
- they SHARE the TEACHING and OBSERVATION in the classroom;
- they EVALUATE the relevance and value of what pupils have gained from each session;
- they REFLECT on what has been learned;
- they USE this in planning the next stage.'

I can't emphasise enough how important these activities are, nor how much hard work is needed on all sides to succeed, nor how important it is that all team members are able to be present at all stages. A share in ownership is important, especially to a student-teacher taking part, to encourage goodwill and continued good input within the team.

The process of planning is very important to give the team a chance to operate. It is the basis for the team spirit and for success. Unfortunately, it seems some teams are restricted by a hidden brief or requirement, by the silent desire of a power within the school to see, for example, more written work. We were fortunate that the ethos and atmosphere in the school allowed for a certain amount of change.

The IT-INSET process is designed to promote the best practice among educators: discussion, co-operation, group work, planning, shared ownership - just what we've been attempting to do for our pupils. The effort involved in, and rewards from, this collaborative work will be high. The emphasis is on learning from everything that is going on around you - from the pupils' responses and from fellow team members. The learning can be almost too much to digest, and yet some gems of the reflection sessions I shall never forget.

Effective collaboration was also the main reason Máire valued the project:

We worked well together because we accepted that we all had strengths and weaknesses, which meant that no-one was in charge and we accepted that we all complemented each other. Working as an equal member of a team was new to me. I must admit that at first I was conscious of the fact that I was a student, Richard a tutor and the teachers exactly that - fully-fledged members of staff at the school. However, this feeling of being watched and wanting to give a good impression which had been so prevalent during teaching practice soon left. We were a team; nobody's contribution was dismissed because of lack of experience.

In typically more expansive, but equally welcome fashion, Keith refers to the experience in the following way:

IT-INSET brings groups of fellow adventurers together to chart a united course. Travelling in numbers can give confidence. Individual abilities, skills and insights can be pooled, while individual tasks can be delegated, later to be fed back into the group. Goals can be discerned more clearly and approached more closely through common effort.

For a time Ian was concerned that genuine, open discussion was not taking place in the team. Perhaps a period of exploring and testing the concept is inevitable. However:

The barriers did drop. The full-time teachers stood back and observed, and when they fed back the usefulness of this I really felt that I was doing something worthwhile and that my opinion was valued. I saw the teachers' role in the team as crucial in initiating the birth of co-operative teamwork. The openness and self-criticism of the whole team helped me to develop a better 'open learning' approach which was tremendously useful in my second teaching practice. The ability to take criticism, indeed the desire for it, and then the ability to use it constructively are the keys to teaching and good practice. Open discussion also gave me confidence to try new techniques, such as drama work, of which I had no real knowledge.

It is hard to put one's finger on why the team was so successful. Some factors I can identify are the honesty of individual team members, the openness of the teaching staff, the commitment and enthusiasm of all of us, and a genuine desire to bring about democratic participation.

Ann was equally enthusiastic about collaboration:

The students enjoyed working as a team and getting away from being students. We were all involved and everyone had something to say and something worth listening to. The teachers placed a great deal of faith in us. It was encouraging to see teachers as just another you or me with the same aims as us.

We enjoyed working together in a real situation and never felt like outsiders who were pushing in. As the programme was cross-curricular we could work in other than our own subjects to try out new ideas and if they did not work there was someone on hand to help us out. By working in small groups for a time we could do more practical things with the pupils. As a team we felt we had been learning the skills which we had been trying to develop in the pupils. We had been able to learn from each other and from the pupils, and found it easy to look at ourselves to ask how we could improve.

Conclusion

Allowing team members to speak for themselves conveys something of the learning power inherent in the IT-INSET process for pupils, students, tutors and teachers. Despite some early reservations, we would all do it again. Not, of course, in exactly the same way: that would not be in the spirit of the process. There were things that we did not get right. For example, we would all have liked more time for evaluation, which because of the school timetable tended to be rushed and interrupted. Some of us would have preferred more work in small groups. Some of us wanted to be more didactic, rather than letting the process evolve. But because we learn from the collaborative process, such differences are helpful as well as being inevitable. 'I would not have missed the experience for anything,' said Ann. 'Like a breath of spring in the middle of a cold winter,' was Eileen's description of the team's presence. 'The benefit to the children has been enormous - that's what I mean by successful INSET,' says the Head of Year.

A balanced conclusion comes from Alan:

At the end of this IT-INSET project, I am more able to discuss, evaluate and see the importance of planning educationally, for the benefit of pupils and myself. The preparation this has been for my final teaching practice and my future career is invaluable. In ten days, over ten weeks, our professional development - especially of the student-teachers - has been remarkable, with so much input from so many different people.

5

Thomas Estley Community College

It is the business of all IT-INSET teams to gather information about their pupils' learning. But not many teams have systematically sought pupils' opinions about what they have done and learned. It is evident from this short case study, drawn from a report compiled by a team working with 12-year-olds in a community college, that children are well able to think critically about their learning and to articulate their views - a capacity of pupils which also emerged in different ways in all of the three previous case studies.

Thomas Estley Community College is a six-form entry community college operating within the Leicestershire system of primary, secondary and upper schools. It is situated in the village of Broughton Astley, about ten miles from Leicester, and receives students from four neighbouring primary schools. The staff of thirty-two is involved not only with statutory provision for students aged 11-14, but also with an extensive community programme, catering for about two thousand adults each week in both day-time and evening classes. The college has a tradition of involvement with initial teacher education in a range of subjects through its links with the Leicester University School of Education.

Following a similar programme in the Spring Term of 1985 (CEDTE 1985), the English Department of Thomas Estley invited the School of Education to support a further IT-INSET programme in the Spring Term of 1986. At meetings held in the Autumn Term between the English staff and a School of Education tutor, the topic - teaching a novel through working and talking in groups - was suggested by the English staff, two of whom had participated in the previous year.

Three teams worked in the school, each composed of a teacher, two students and a tutor. Each team concentrated on a different novel. All three employed group work, but they experimented with a variety of methods including group discussion, three-minute talks in pairs, role-play of incidents drawn from the novels, dramatised readings, and balloon debates.

An extract from a team report provides their evaluation of their activities.

> *Worthwhileness* We concluded that the worthwhile aspects were:
> - pupils' gains in courage to talk and respond publicly;
> - their having a go at one-to-one communication over a prolonged period;
> - their more mature form of teamwork in organising the role-play.
>
> *What did we learn?* We began to think we had learned something about:
> - when *not* to intervene (after rather than during an interchange);
> - what pupils like to talk about;
> - the importance of choosing topics that relate to all members of a group;
> - the need to make our aims explicit;
> - the value of pupils seeing us getting involved in the same activities - showing that we're not infallible;
> - pupils achieving more when talking through others, as in role-play;
> - the many factors which influence pupils' involvement in discussion.

The views of pupils

In order to investigate and evaluate children's responses to the IT-INSET work, one team devised a written questionnaire which each child answered.

Out of twenty-three replies, only two pupils were overtly critical of the Tuesday sessions: they neither enjoyed them nor found them beneficial. One of these, a confident extrovert girl, found she did not like group work and preferred to work alone. The other twenty-one all seemed to find Tuesday mornings 'enjoyable' and 'different'. The reasons for their evident enjoyment were fairly similar. The majority expressed a liking for working in small groups which included discussions and various group tasks. Many had had only limited experience of group work of this nature before.

But did the children, in addition to enjoying the work, find it beneficial in any way? Certainly the shy retiring types were of the opinion that it helped their confidence tremendously and enhanced their social and communication skills. One said that she had 'learned that I am shy and I am not very shy any more because of these lessons.' Another said that she had 'learned to talk better in a group.' One quiet boy said, 'I don't usually speak in groups but I do now.'

A number of children felt that working in small groups added to their confidence. They felt more secure and relaxed working within this kind of framework. One particularly shy boy said that in a small group he felt less nervous about saying the wrong thing and another boy said that 'a small group was bestest.'

It is interesting to note that a number of children felt that group work had a positive part to play in other subjects in the curriculum, in particular mathematics, the humanities, music and science. One girl mentioned that working in small groups 'can give you confidence, say like in maths.' However, another child who had experience of group work in mathematics said, 'We did group work in maths, but that was rubbish.' He thought it more appropriate and enjoyable in English.

According to the majority of pupils, group work enabled them to share experiences and pool ideas. Discussion was central to their perception of benefit, as for one boy who said, 'You can say what you think but you can't always write down what you think.' One child found it useful to work in groups 'so we could help each other out.'

A further question asked whether the pupils gained a better understanding of the book they were studying through group work. It seems that many found it useful to discuss aspects of the book as a group, and some said that 'talking' helped them to enjoy the book more. As one child said, 'I think the way we have read it and done bits of work from it has helped me.' Another boy reinforced this idea: 'The lessons have helped me to look more deeply into what I read.' On the whole, discussion seemed to enhance enjoyment of the book. One pupil who is an excellent conversationalist but a weak writer remarked, 'I enjoyed the book because we didn't just sit and read it.' In addition, a number of children commented that, as a result of the detailed work they had done in class together on *Carrie's War* by Nina Bawden, they had learned more about what it must have been like to have been an evacuee.

The majority of children expressed a liking for the role-play lessons, perhaps because they felt less inhibited playing parts. Many of them commented favourably on the lesson on 'fear', which was based entirely on discussion in both smaller and larger groups. For one child, it was a chance 'to speak out'.

The last question was what pupils thought of the four adult members present in their Tuesday sessions. Most thought that the students were there to 'help out' or to 'gain experience' and to 'see what being a teacher is all about' in order eventually to 'become qualified teachers'. Many pupils thought that the class teacher's role was to supervise the students (or to have a 'rest') and that the tutor was there to observe them and 'take down notes'. Some children expressed discomfort at being observed by the team. As one child said, 'The thing I didn't like was being watched and people writing down what we said.' One child thought that the four adults were present so that they 'know how children of our age react to certain things and how we cope with the work we have been set.' Another said that the team were there to teach them 'how to talk in small groups and monitor our reactions to talking and working in groups.'

It seems that the majority of children did enjoy the Tuesday sessions, partly because 'we all get together' and partly because 'we do different things'. Many of the academically weak and less communicative pupils found the experience valuable to their progress and social development. Even the girl who was most critical of the scheme claimed that, though she had 'not learned anything' from these lessons, 'other members of the class have learned to speak out instead of being shy.'

6

College of Ripon and York St John

John Lee, Director of Teacher Education Programmes at the College of Ripon and York St John, wrote the following account of the college's extensive preparations for IT-INSET. The College has been a relative late-comer to IT-INSET and has thus benefited from the experience accumulated in other training institutions. Review of ten years of IT-INSET suggests that there is no accidental relationship between the thoroughness and care with which the preparatory work was undertaken by this College and its Local Education Authority and the perceived success of its first programme.

The College of Ripon and York St John is a voluntary college, formed in 1975 by the amalgamation of two Church of England Colleges - The College, Ripon, and St John's College, York. The campuses are 25 miles apart.

In 1975 there were 1,500 teacher education students; the College is now a diversified institution with nearly 2,000 students, offering modular BEd, BA and BSc degrees validated by Leeds University. The intake in primary teacher education is 140 honours BEd students and forty post-graduate certificate in education students; in secondary teacher education there are honours BEd students in design and technology, mathematics and religious education, and post-graduate certificate in education students in design and technology.

The College has a long tradition of in-service work with teachers. From 1975, in co-operation with North Yorkshire Local Education Authority, it has housed teachers' centres at Ripon and York and a language centre at Ripon. As well as consultancy work in schools, the College offers a range of certificates, advanced diplomas and masters' degrees, also validated by the University of Leeds.

The introduction to IT-INSET

In the autumn of 1978, the College sent its Directors of Initial Teacher Training and In-service Teacher Training to an IT-INSET conference at the Open University. They concluded that the time was not appropriate to introduce the IT-INSET model into the existing validated BEd degree and that staffing, at one tutor to six students, was not financially feasible.

However, during 1983 and 1984 the College went through the process of revalidating its primary honours BEd degree with the University of Leeds.

Concurrently the institution was being inspected by Her Majesty's Inspectors. Among other evidence and advice looked at by the College was a visit by Pat Ashton, the Director of the Centre for Evaluation and Development in Teacher Education, to talk to college staff involved in teacher education about the value of the IT-INSET model - its benefits to students and staff and its potential for in-service development in schools. As a result of this visit, the college's working party on the primary BEd and senior staff concerned with teacher education began to explore the possibility of incorporating IT-INSET within the developing modular pattern of the new degree.

If partnership between students, teachers and tutors was to be an important criterion for the effective operation of IT-INSET teams, it was felt that a course in the third year would be the most appropriate time for students to engage in IT-INSET. At the end of their first year, and again towards the end of their second year, students would have three-week and six-week school practices, the latter requiring them to teach all the subjects in the primary curriculum. At the beginning of the second year they would also take a course including a section on classroom observation skills.

By the third year, therefore, students should have relevant subject knowledge, curriculum knowledge, experience of working with children in their academic area of study, and the beginnings of the skills of classroom observation. It was thought that this would give them status alongside a tutor who would have both subject and curriculum strengths but not necessarily recent contact with children. It would also give them status alongside a class teacher who would have a wealth of understanding of the children in the school, and her class in particular, but not necessarily the recent curriculum development opportunities enjoyed by the students and college staff.

The aspiration

If the model were successful, it was envisaged that IT-INSET would bring the following benefits.

For the students, it would:
- ensure that they maintained contact with the classroom, since the third year of the BEd course does not include a formal school practice;
- enable them to work in small groups using observation skills;
- give them a deeper understanding of how their own subject strength could be developed in the classroom;
- enable them to develop negotiating skills within the team, including whole-team planning of curriculum development, relevant to their final school practice and subsequently;
- give them opportunities to act as chairperson and secretary of a meeting.

For the teachers, it would:
- enable them to develop, with a team, one particular aspect of the primary curriculum of common concern;
- enable them to develop skills of classroom observation;
- give them a chance to stand back from their own class and discuss with other professionals their observations of how children respond;
- give them the opportunity to be deeply involved in initial teacher training;
- give them the chance to meet other teachers similarly involved.

For the college staff, it would:
- give them the opportunity to work in their own curriculum area with primary children;
- help them to develop their classroom observation skills, and thus develop their ablity to help students in school practice situations;
- give them the opportunity to develop a more sustained relationship with a class and a school than is possible in normal school practice situations;
- enable them to participate, with the team, in planning the work.

For the children,
- the concentration of so much expertise would immediately benefit the classes of children involved;

• the increased awareness of all concerned would benefit other classes in the future.

The participants

The *students* would all be third-year primary honours BEd students who had successfully completed two school practices. They would be grouped according to their academic subject - art, geography, history, human movement, language/literature (English or French), mathematics, music, religious education, and science (biology, chemistry or rural science). They would be studying a course within Part II of their degree programme which for one day per week of the semester investigated the nature of their subject - its place in the primary curriculum, what might be taught, and how this might be taught[1]. For the other day per week of the course they would be in school, working as members of an IT-INSET team.

The *tutors* would mainly be members of the academic subject areas with a professional interest in the primary school curriculum. The college departmental structure is such that several of the professional curriculum courses are taught by members of subject departments who have qualified teacher status. Many of these were initially trained to teach in secondary schools and, although many have already spent considerable time working in primary schools, it was felt that involvement in IT-INSET would provide valuable additional experience, particularly in the light of the emphasis placed by the Department of Education and Science on recent school teaching experience (DES 1984). In a three-year rolling programme, it is intended that all tutors involved in supervision of primary school practice and in curriculum courses will have taken part in the IT-INSET programme. These tutors would be responsible for the day in College as well as being involved in school-based teams. Additional members of the subject departments, as well as members of the Professional Studies Department, would be involved in the school-based work to achieve the staffing ratio of not more than six students to one tutor or class.

The *schools* involved would, in the first instance, all be in the North Yorkshire Education Authority and there would need to be both formal and informal meetings with officers and advisers of the Authority before schools were approached. Schools for the first year of IT-INSET would be selected from those which already had contact with the College in at least one of the following ways:

- through school practice (in an average year the College involves 200 North Yorkshire schools as well as schools in Bradford, Cleveland, Doncaster, Humberside and Leeds);
- through 'school experience', i.e. students working on activities with small groups of children (courses in all four years of the primary honours BEd involve schools in this way);
- consultancy by college staff on specific curriculum areas;
- teachers on long in-service courses at the College;
- staff acting as teacher tutors (for the last four years the College, in conjunction with North Yorkshire Education Authority, has employed seven teacher tutors for one day per week to teach on college courses).

There would need to be meetings with each school to obtain their agreement to being involved in what would be a new venture for both the College and themselves, in the context of already considerable pressures for other course and school practice placements.

The programme of action

Successful implementation of IT-INSET requires very careful planning and preparation. At the College of Ripon and York St John, the planning phase lasted for two years, from the autumn of 1985 to implementation in the autumn of 1987. Preparation was required within the college's decision-making processes and with college staff, with the Local Education Authority, with individual schools, and with students. Table 6.1 on pages 83-86 sets out some of the key points in the planning process.

Preparation within the College
An initial planning meeting was held in September 1985 between Alan Peacock of the Centre for Evaluation and Development in Teacher Education, who was to become the college's 'mentor' in the exercise, and the Director of Teacher Education Programmes, along with one of the tutors responsible for the development of classroom observation skills. Its purpose was to explore how:

- students could further develop their classroom observation skills from the stage reached in their second-year course;
- staff could be involved, by providing a short course on

observation skills and class interaction;
• the Local Education Authority might best be involved.

A series of visits to institutions already involved in IT-INSET was arranged for college staff. The first of these took place in November, when the Head of Professional Studies and the Director of Teacher Education Programmes visited Middlesex Polytechnic and one of its IT-INSET schools. In the following two years, college staff visited several other IT-INSET institutions.

During the spring of 1986 a paper on the staffing of IT-INSET went the rounds of college committees, finally obtaining the approval of the Academic Board for the exceptional staffing of the school-based work. It was evident that the newly validated honours BEd degree would make greater demands on staff time, particularly for the staff of main subject departments, as well as for those tutors who were involved in the studies advisory programme[2]. It was also already apparent that, with the introduction of Grant-Related In-Service Training (GRIST) in April 1987, there would be no money in the college in-service budget for the exceptional staffing of IT-INSET.

In March, Alan Peacock met the college staff likely to be involved in the exercise (as well as one of North Yorkshire's primary advisers) to discuss other institutions' experience of IT-INSET and to try to allay any anxieties the staff might be developing. The discussion focused particularly on IT-INSET's role in relation to the requirement for recent relevant experience.

In October, a number of college staff attended a national conference on *Subject studies in IT-INSET*, and in November the College, with North Yorkshire Local Education Authority, jointly hosted a further national conference on *Planning and preparation for IT-INSET*. Over a hundred people attended, representing eighteen training institutions and twelve local education authorities, and including headteachers, teachers, tutors, college co-ordinators, students and advisers. Besides hosting the conference, many college staff attended, including at least one member of each department involved, as well as representatives of the student body, including the Academic Affairs Officers of both campuses.

In February 1987 the college's Professional Advisory and Accreditation Board was briefed on the progress of IT-INSET, and in March Alan Peacock visited the College again to discuss the programme on observation skills for schools and tutors that would take place in the summer.

Planning with the local education authority
In April 1986 the Director and Deputy Director of Teacher Education Programmes met the primary advisers in whose areas the IT-INSET programme would take place. For the first implementation of IT-INSET, the following points were agreed.

- A range of large and small schools would be involved.
- Schools would be chosen which were known to be sympathetic both to the College and to curriculum innovation.
- An attempt would be made to group schools geographically to facilitate transport of students.
- Both the College and the local education authority would be involved in the evaluation of the school-based work.
- The whole exercise would be reviewed after the first term of school-based work and the criteria for selection of schools would then be reconsidered.

Following this initial discussion, there were several further meetings with staff of the North Yorkshire Education Authority. In June, Alan Peacock and the Directorate of Teacher Education Programmes spoke to all the advisers and an area education officer about IT-INSET. In November, the Director of Teacher Education Programmes addressed the North Yorkshire INSET Committee, and later in the same month the Principal and other senior staff of the College met the Deputy Chief Education Officer and Chief Adviser for North Yorkshire to discuss the future of in-service education, including IT-INSET, under GRIST funding. In December, the Director of Teacher Education Programmes spoke about the IT-INSET model to the Harrogate Teachers' Centre Committee.

Planning with the schools
By the summer of 1987, potential schools had been identified. Initially the advisers made contact with them by letter, offering the opportunity for each school to meet either the Director or Deputy Director of Teacher Education Programmes. The aim of these meetings would be to answer questions, solve problems and allay fears. All schools took up this offer and a full staff meeting was held in each one. The following main points of concern were raised.

- How was IT-INSET to be organised?
- How would the children cope with seven additional adults in the classroom?

- How would the team cope in the physical space available?
- Where was the in-service benefit? Was IT-INSET not really serial teaching practice by another name?
- Why did it have to be subject-based in an integrated situation? (In practice, although all the teams were subject-specific, the subject was taught within an integrated day where this was more appropriate.)
- Which team would be involved in their school?

At this stage two schools, out of a total of sixteen, decided to withdraw and had to be replaced.

In June, the first of two meetings took place for all school and college staff who would be involved in IT-INSET the following term, discussing the model in general and the development of classroom observation skills in particular. These two-hour sessions gave the teachers and tutors the opportunity to meet each other, although some pairings were still not settled.

Preparing the students
The first briefings of students who were to engage in IT-INSET in the autumn took place at the Ripon campus in January 1987 and at the York campus in February. The timing of these was to enable students to register by March for courses beginning in the following academic year. Although the BEd programmes are linear, some choice is available within curriculum options and these are discussed by the Directorate of Teacher Education Programmes with the students. In June, a further opportunity was created for students to talk in more detail about IT-INSET.

The position reached at the start of work in school

Work accomplished
- All the relevant committees and boards within the college's decision-making structure were fully informed and had given all the necessary approvals.
- Two years of planning and preparation inside the College had achieved, for the staff involved, a gradual build-up of their understanding and confidence.
- Close collaboration with North Yorkshire Education Authority had enabled schools to be identified, and the Authority had made a firm commitment to the release of each class teacher involved to

take part in team discussions by making supply teachers available for the afternoons of each of the days the teams would be in schools.

- Meetings with school staffs and between class teachers and college tutors over the previous six months had developed an awareness of the implications of IT-INSET for the schools.
- Students had been given some preparation for their involvement, particularly in the development of observation skills, although it was in the three weeks in September before the start of work in schools that students' preparation was completed.

Points of concern
These included:
- whether the academic standard of the work would be appropriate for Part II of the honours BEd degree;
- the high staffing and transport costs, and the limited time students would be in school (not arriving before 10.30 am and having to leave by 2.30 pm);
- apprehension on the part of some college staff who were unsure about the full implications of their role in teams;
- apprehension on the part of class teachers and concern from some headteachers who could see the benefits to students but were less certain about the in-service benefits;
- uncertainty about the effects on children of eight adults in the classroom;
- a feeling on the part of students that, since this was the first time the College had been involved in IT-INSET, they were acting as guinea-pigs.

The programme in practice

One day each week for thirteen weeks was set aside in the Autumn Term for IT-INSET. The first three were college-based, involving the class teacher coming into College so that members of the team could get to know one another and decide who would teach what - and how - in the first session in school. In practice, all teams actually went into schools on the second or third of these days to meet the children.

There then followed the eight sessions in school (interrupted by the schools' half-term holiday which was used for consolidation of ideas). The programme of a typical day was:

10.00 am	Leave College
10.30 am	Arrive at school - team preparation
11.00 am	Teaching/observing session
12 noon	Lunch followed by team discussion
2.30 pm	Return to College

Each team elected a chairperson and secretary as well as the person to teach for each week. Over the eight weeks every team member had a chance to teach, to observe, and to act as chairperson and secretary. The secretary circulated minutes to all team members, with copies to the Directorate of Teacher Education Programmes. These minutes contained details of the observations made in the classroom, the team's discussion of them, and planning for the following week.

During the weeks in school, the teams were visited by advisers, a member of Her Majesty's Inspectorate, and the Director and Deputy Director of Teacher Education Programmes.

The students were required to keep a diary of what happened in the classroom, as well as to complete the evaluation booklets provided by the Centre for Evaluation and Development in Teacher Education (Appendices 5, 6 and 7). From these resources, and the minutes of team meetings, each student was asked to write an assignment on the learning needs of the children, the learning activities undertaken, and the appropriateness of the teaching strategies employed.

The final meetings of the teams took place in College after the Christmas vacation, when both the class teacher and the tutor assessed and graded the students' records of the school-based work and the teams reviewed their work and collectively completed the evaluation booklet. Alan Peacock was in College on that day to observe and to talk with teams, as well as to participate in a meeting of all the teachers and tutors involved to review the semester's work.

Also in the spring, the team whose subject had been human movement made a presentation to the college's In-service Committee, and one of the religious education teams addressed the college's Professional Advisory and Accreditation Board.

Evaluation

The data available for evaluation consisted of the evaluation booklets completed by all team members, students' assignments, observation by non-participants of the work done in schools, and the evaluation meeting of teachers, tutors and students. All of these varied perceptions demonstrated that the IT-INSET model can work - and work well - in meeting the aspirations of the various members of the teams.

The aspirations for the students were more than met. The work they produced for assessment was of a good academic standard, and some was highly perceptive. Their increased confidence and deepened perceptions will serve them well in their final school practice and beyond. The following are some examples of students' own views of the benefits:

Discussion triggers your own ideas on the learning taking place.
Working as a team helps you discover your own good and bad points.
You get a chance to see how children develop over a whole term.
The chance to work in close contact with a small group of children and to watch, record and evaluate their reactions.
Speaking to teachers and tutors as an equal.
Allows students to teach without feeling under the pressure of assessment.

That the teachers' aspirations were met is demonstrated by their schools' desire to be involved again, as well as by comments like:

The main advantage for me was that I could observe the children in a more detached way.
I have learned a great deal through the experience, especially working as a team, sharing ideas.
The opportunity not only to talk about ideas but to put them into practice and gauge the children's responses so closely was unique.

Those headteachers who had earlier been doubtful about the in-service benefits of IT-INSET were now convinced.

The aspirations of tutors have also been met in most cases, and enthusiasm runs high. The following are typical of tutors' views of the benefits to them:

I became almost part of the school staff instead of rushing in
and then hurrying off to the next appointment.
The opportunity to work with a team.
The chance to teach a class.
More space and time for reflection on children's learning.
The level of discussion reached remarkable depths.

Above all, the evaluation showed, in the vast majority of teams,
the integration of the team. By the end of the term's work members
of teams were relaxed in one another's company and were prepared to
share ideas freely. On the other hand, most teams still had some way
to go in the analysis of practice, the application of theory and the
evaluation of the curriculum. These will need more attention in the
college's next IT-INSET programme. Also, students need an earlier
understanding of the full aims of the exercise and of the purpose and
form of the assessment. The problem of shortage of time was
commented on by almost all participants, but this will be difficult
to solve because of the effect on the programme of the allocation of
hours specified in *Circular 3/84* (DES 1984) and the financial
constraints on transport.

Postscript

The survey by Her Majesty's Inspectorate *Quality in schools* (DES
1987c) comments:

> Serial attachment, particularly where tutor, class teacher and
> students worked together in the classroom, emerged from the
> survey as a very valuable aspect of training and as one of the
> most positive features of relationships with schools.

IT-INSET has shown itself to be such in the comments of
participants and the reports of others. But the experience at the
College of Ripon and York St John has been more than this. At the
final evaluation meeting, a teacher said that she 'had learned more in
one term of IT-INSET than in ten years of teaching.' The meeting
was remarkable for the fact that, even in this quite large gathering,
there was no negative comment. In a case study written by the
organisers of an IT-INSET programme who are understandably
concerned with the important details of planning and execution, it is

always difficult to allow what another teacher called the 'magic' of the experience to show through. What does emerge is how well the first attempt at IT-INSET by this College went. Another small but significant indicator is that the first get-together of participants for the autumn 1988 programme had a 100 per cent attendance of tutors and teachers for an evening meeting. The fact that the programme went so well is a tribute to the college's thorough planning (and excellent hospitality) and to the active support of the Local Education Authority and its schoools throughout the previous two years.

Immediately after the 1987 programme had ended, the Directorate of Teacher Education Programmes and local education authority advisers met to plan the 1988 programme. This immediately established a commitment to continuing and improving IT-INSET. But it must not lose its edge and sparkle - its 'magic' - by becoming routine. New schools and different teachers, tutors and students will be involved in 1988 and these, alongside experienced participants, should help to keep perceptions fresh. Ultimately, the programme may extend to other local education authorities also.

Notes

1. The college year is divided into two semesters. Students take two courses each semester, and thus a total of sixteen courses in the four-year honours BEd, of which the IT-INSET project is one.

2. The studies advisory programme occurs on Wednesdays throughout the four years of the honours BEd except when students are on school practice, and is additional to the two courses per semester. The work includes school visits, some initial curriculum work, work on economic awareness, health education and multicultural education, as well as programme guidance, preparation for school practice and supervision.

Table 6.1   Key points in the planning process

Date	College	LEA	Schools	Students
Sept 1985	CEDTE mentor meets DTEP and tutor responsible for development of classroom observation skills			
Oct 1985	CEDTE mentor meets senior College staff to plan visits to other IT-INSET institutions			
Nov 1985	CEDTE mentor and senior College staff to Middlesex Polytechnic			

/cont.

Date	College	LEA	Schools	Students
Spring Term 1986	Paper on staffing of IT-INSET goes rounds of College committees			
Apr 1986		DTEP meets primary advisers in whose areas IT-INSET is to take place		
Jun 1986	CEDTE mentor meets College staff likely to be involved and one of the primary advisers to discuss IT-INSET model and experience in other institutions			
Oct 1986	College staff attend national conference on subject studies in IT-INSET			

/cont.

Date	College	LEA	Schools	Students
Nov 1986	College and North Yorkshire LEA jointly host national conference *Planning and preparation for IT-INSET*			
Nov 1986		DTEP addresses North Yorkshire INSET Committee		
Nov 1986		Senior College and LEA staff discuss effect of GRIST on IT-INSET		
Nov 1986	Meeting of College Committee to discuss academic year 1987/88 - staffing and transport costs of IT-INSET			

/cont.

Date	College	LEA	Schools	Students
Dec 1986		DTEP meets Harrogate Teachers' Centre Committee in whose area part of programme will happen		
Jan 1987				DTEP speaks to Ripon students who will be involved
Feb 1987				DTEP speaks to York students who will be involved
Feb 1987	College Professional Advisory and Accreditation Board briefed on progress			

/cont.

Date	College	LEA	Schools	Students
Mar 1987	CEDTE mentor discusses with College staff programme of observational skills for Summer Term			
Apr 1987			Beginning of a series of meetings between DTEP and individual school staffs	
Jun 1987				Further meeting with students
Jun 1987			All school and College staff meet to discuss IT-INSET model and observation skills	

7

Leicestershire Education Authority

This case study exemplifies collaboration between a local education authority and a training institution. Local education authority officers are notoriously hard-pressed, and it was therefore compiled from a tape-recording of an interview with Brian Cruickshank, Leicestershire's INSET Co-ordinator, conducted by a member of staff of Leicester University's School of Education. This device has made it possible to quote Brian Cruickshank at length, while also enlarging the context to encompass the School of Education's role in the partnership.

While IT-INSET has been very occasionally introduced to a training institution by its local education authority, the reverse is almost universally the case. The college or university department approaches the local education authority with, at the least, a request for permission to offer IT-INSET to local schools or, at the most, a request for a collaborative working partnership in the planning and conduct of the programme. Of all the collaborative relationships which IT-INSET requires, that between the local education authority and the training institution is perhaps the most difficult to achieve. While they share the ultimate aim of serving the educational purposes of pupils, their short-term objectives and daily preoccupations are distinctly different. Roles, tasks, responsibilities and stresses are quite dissimilar and create different professional climates, and even languages, in County Hall and the college.

The Grant-Related In-Service Training (GRIST) arrangements, while expanding opportunities for diverse forms of INSET, have also brought a flavour of the market place to the relationships between local education authorities and training institutions, with selective buying and selling of expertise replacing a kind of relaxed professional negotiation. Moreover, the working partnership between college and local education authority almost inevitably lacks the sustained and regular contact which tends greatly to facilitate other dyads and triads in IT-INSET.

The best possible collaboration between local education authority and training institution must be the goal of IT-INSET planners. Unless both agencies are in some way visible in the schools where IT-INSET is practised, it is difficult for headteachers and teachers to overturn the assumption that IT-INSET is simply the latest fashionable name for students' school experience. This is particularly true now that GRIST has tended to increase every teacher's consciousness of the local education authority's planning, provision and evaluation of INSET. IT-INSET needs to be seen as a genuine INSET option. If, better still, the teachers involved are to be provided with supply cover so that they can play a full part in the evaluation sessions, to the benefit of themselves and the rest of their teams, then the local education authority must first have placed an appropriate value on IT-INSET. Furthermore, if the IT-INSET process and its curriculum development products are to spread and multiply between schools, then it is essential that the local education authority shares its overview of in-service policy and planning with the training institution.

The outcomes of collaboration between local education authority and training institution are much easier to define than the forms they might take. These will vary for many reasons, from historical relationships to the personalities involved. There is unlikely to be a blueprint for effective collaboration, but a critical examination of one case may illuminate the issues to be considered. The collaboration between the School of Education of the University of Leicester and Leicestershire Local Education Authority is essentially *ad hoc*, combining a lack of joint organisation with a shared responsiveness. The following account is substantially drawn from a tape-recorded conversation with Leicestershire's INSET Co-ordinator, Brian Cruickshank, who is the School of Education's prime contact in respect of IT-INSET.

The context for collaboration

IT-INSET was first practised by Leicester University School of Education on a very limited scale in 1981 and a handful of interested tutors began to experiment with the programme over the following four years. An IT-INSET Co-ordinator (Secondary) was nominated in 1985, closely followed by one for the primary course. From that date, IT-INSET expanded rapidly and now involves almost every tutor.

Prior to the establishment of IT-INSET, the School of Education set up an MA(Ed) course in teacher education, and this later became significant in the growth of IT-INSET for two reasons. First, the course is based on the principles and practice of IT-INSET and, while primarily oriented to preparing students for a leading role in in-service education, it became a vital source of additional tutors for IT-INSET programmes. Secondly, the course was the cause of irregular but sustained contact between the course leader and Brian Cruickshank: he was consulted about its design, takes part every year in interviewing applicants, and makes a significant practical contribution to regional advertising and facilitating the post-course activities of students. The course is an important key to this particular local education authority/training institution collaboration because it gives rise to joint, purposeful and practical activity. Pure discussion meetings between parties with a dozen other preoccupations can elicit a very low level of real attention to issues. Selecting candidates for scarce full-time secondments and matching local education authority and university criteria obliges the parties to expose their judgements and clarify their purposes. The precise nature of the joint activity is not important; it is critical that it has a practical outcome which depends upon mutual understanding.

A joint, purposeful activity also provides continuing opportunities for a great deal of incidental talk. Anyone involved in IT-INSET knows how difficult it is to convey its principles and the nature of its practice. Moreover, the perspective of the local education authority is inevitably different from that of the training institution and the differences need to be appreciated by both partners. Mutual understanding seems more readily negotiated over time and in conditions in which abstract concepts are associated with practical examples. For instance, a secondary school chose to use the IT-INSET supply cover to release, not the teacher involved to take part in the discussion, but the head of department to join the team. This was irritating from the point of view of the School of Education but came to make sense when it emerged through discussion later that Brian Cruickshank placed a higher priority on institutionalising IT-INSET in this particular situation than on the quality of the individual programme. This piecing together and extending of mutual understanding of IT-INSET and its role in the development both of schools and of the initial training course seems to emerge best from continuing and practical co-operative work.

Practicalities

No-one can remember exactly when the critical conversation took place that resulted in Leicestershire providing supply cover at the rate of half a day per teacher per IT-INSET day. It certainly occurred in the course of one of the incidental discussions and arose from an unpremeditated suggestion from the MA course leader, at a point where it seemed to be a natural consequence of what was being said, leading to instant agreement on Brian Cruickshank's part. Such a decision is a major plank in establishing IT-INSET in a local education authority. Teams are enabled to function properly with full attendance at a substantial meeting each week; teachers recognise IT-INSET as an important form of INSET; IT-INSET appears in the local education authority's budget and figures in its GRIST submission; the programme becomes accountable and changes from merely an additional, interesting offering from the School of Education to a local education authority practice subject to monitoring and evaluation and expected to show results.

How did it come about that Brian Cruickshank agreed without hesitation to seek to provide cover and has not only delivered the then agreed figure of £5,000 but has increased it annually to a current figure of around £12,000 in line with the increase in the amount of IT-INSET on offer from the School of Education? In practical terms, his particular role as INSET Co-ordinator is of enormous assistance. As a central figure in Leicestershire's INSET planning, he was able to prepare a report on IT-INSET and ensure that it figured on the agenda of the INSET Working Group whose membership includes county councillors, education officers, and advisers. Following a brief discussion, the budget was approved: IT-INSET had become institutionalised. In ways such as this, Brian Cruickshank provides the School of Education with a single point of contact and saves the dissipation of time and information which so often accompanies tortuous routes through committees or a chain of individuals with different responsibilities. However, as he said:

When I came to Leicestershire over a decade ago, I was the second such appointment nationally. Most local education authorities now have someone in post with something roughly equivalent to my job. I would think that, up and down the country, it ought now to be very much easier for institutions to link up with one or two individuals or to have access to the equivalent of their own professional advisory committee on INSET.

The original approval of funding for IT-INSET occurred before the arrival of GRIST. But having been established as part of Leicestershire's INSET provision, IT-INSET was absorbed into the GRIST budget as an item in the 'local priority area' category, as part of a programme described as 'Classroom evaluation/IT-INSET/active learning'. Brian Cruickshank now thinks, however:

In my view it should not appear in one of the programmes but rather should be spread across all the programmes, especially the second and third of our main programme blocks, 'cross curriculum' and 'subject/course programmes'. This would facilitate wider awareness of IT-INSET within the advisory service.

Shared philosophy

It is one thing to have the authority to support IT-INSET practically, however, and another to have the will. It is here that consonance between local education authority and training institution in their philosophies of teacher education is fundamental to any kind of progress. Undoubtedly, Leicester University School of Education has been fortunate. It is worth quoting Brian Cruickshank at length because his philosophy and its practical implications demonstrate fertile ground for IT-INSET.

IT-INSET is very central. It's focused on practice, focused on what is happening in classrooms - what pupils are doing, and what teachers are trying to do with them. If I had any overriding aim or intention, it would be just that. It seems self-evident that in-service education is about really meeting the needs of children through meeting the needs of staff: IT-INSET is, *per se*, a good thing. It seems to me self-evident that if you are involving a group of professionals in the working life of a group of youngsters that's bound, broadly speaking, to pay dividends. The difficult bits are when you get into whether their learning has actually improved. Is it broadly beneficial? Yes, I guess that's what's happened in Leicestershire; teachers have been broadly aware that it is beneficial for youngsters because the pupils have been happier. They've been engaging with a group of adults and we probably all find that difficult to pin down in terms of improved children's learning. We probably now all ought to be involved in trying to collect some evidence, not just in IT-INSET, but in all INSET - some data which would help us to decide whether INSET is associated with improved learning.

It is interesting that a central tenet of IT-INSET, evaluating children's learning, has actually emerged for Brian Cruickshank as an obvious development from teams simply working collaboratively with children, which he has regarded as of major value in itself. It is here that a distinctive local education authority perspective is apparent, with a view of general changes in attitudes and practices which would be desirable in the schools. Brian Cruickshank emphasised the importance for him both of children being involved in INSET activities and of teachers collaborating. He went on:

There is still a fair reluctance to engage children in the process. I guess if we actually got a group of teachers together and said this would be a good thing, they would applaud the idea. They would also see other aspects of in-service as being important, like career development and getting qualifications. But, by and large, nobody would disagree with involving chidren. Yet it still isn't widely practised. I suppose I've been out of schools too long now to know precisely why it isn't, but I guess it's something to do with classrooms still being somewhat closed, institutions being somewhat closed, teachers often not sharing with colleagues. It's threatening to have others working in the classroom, especially if the general mode of teaching is didactic. There's not much to share - or perhaps there is really if you dig down, but it's very threatening. Probably if just a few of the scales were lifted, even the most didactic, with a bit of prising and probing, would admit that they're not quite certain what they're up to and are really quite uncertain about many things that are going on, or not going on, in the children's learning. It's easy to go on pretending.

Institutionalisation

Leicestershire's commitment to developing school-focused INSET predated the advent of IT-INSET, as did Brian Cruikshank's personal conviction that in-service education should contribute directly to pupils' experience, although, as he said, it is difficult to say precisely how this is manifested:

> Leicestershire has a long tradition of giving schools autonomy. The advisory service has always been regarded as school-focused. Advisers and officers have been encouraged to get into schools as much as possible. The teachers' centres have always worked closely with local schools. Advisory teachers have been appointed to develop ideas. There has always been a view in the Authority, and quite a widespread one, that INSET is most effective when it gets closest to the classroom. In practice, however, we have only recently - within the last two or three years - really begun to get a grip on what this means. IT-INSET has been one of the influences, albeit a rather small influence, on these developments. The major large-scale influences have been, in my view, TRIST[1] - which gave birth to the area collaborative INSET, Grant-Related In-Service Training - which involved surveying school needs, professional tutor work[2], and the school-focused work arising out of the MA in Teacher Education.

Still, however, Brian Cruickshank recognises the difficulty in cultivating an understanding in schools of what school-focused INSET in general, and IT-INSET in particular, really means in practice. Reviewing its development in Leicestershire, he said:

There have been tremendous moves over the last two or three years, but it's not widespread. The professional tutor development over the last two terms has shown how far we are from achieving enormous strides, although great progress has been made. At the beginning of the professional tutor programme, in September 1987, the majority of staff still tended to look at INSET as something out there that was done to them. Through the good work of the professional tutors - though you may ask why it hadn't happened before - through the injection of money and time, staff are being brought round to see INSET as something they do for themselves. It's difficult to generalise, but it's probably still very patchy. In the same way, many of them simply do not know what the curriculum review process means[3]. If they've not been involved in reviewing the curriculum themselves, they have this document arriving on their desks which is all about curriculum review and it's just words on a page. Similarly, Tony Gelsthorpe's report[4], which is also in all schools, is words on a page about IT-INSET. There's a very real sense in which it only becomes important and written into their practice if they've had some contact with it. IT-INSET has made a significant contribution in those schools where it has been practised. But it's not as widespread, on as wide a front, as I would like.

IT-INSET is thus seen as meeting an identified need in Leicestershire and is supported in principle. Like any other local education authority, Leicestershire is accountable for its INSET spending and, since it meets a defined need, IT-INSET is regarded as good value. Indeed:

> It's pretty cheap in-service. In very simplistic terms, for £12,000 we're getting forty-odd teachers involved on a developmental basis each term. So for the equivalent of one year's secondment, we've got forty teachers involved across a term and forty by three is more or less equivalent to ten full-time secondments for £12,000. I can't imagine that teachers see an IT-INSET programme as simply a series of one-offs, one session per week. They'll be thinking between times, there'll be an impact on them, they'll be preparing that much more carefully, thinking about things because they know that on a particular afternoon something's going to be happening. So I would think we're getting much, much more than half a day's INSET involvement for them. Many of them are getting quite excited, doing an awful lot of thinking about it both before and after IT-INSET is actually happening, and probably discussing it with colleagues.

Progress in collaboration

Leicestershire Education Authority and Leicester University School of Education enjoy an informal collaboration in IT-INSET. It works on a basis of shared principles and reasonably easy communication - perhaps the fact that many tutors and advisers solve the problems of contacting one another by ringing one another at home in the evenings is a not unimportant symbol of the relationships that exist. The Local Education Authority endorses the principles of IT-INSET, welcomes it, and is prepared to put money into it. Leicestershire and the School of Education are learning to understand one another's perspectives. It is interesting to speculate, however, whether full collaboration should also involve a willingness to take one another's perspectives into account. Brian Cruickshank is unequivocal on this point:

> I don't look at it at all from the point of view of initial training. As I regard it, if there's a spin-off for the initial training students, all well and good, but primarily it's INSET as far as I'm concerned.

Though, having said that:

> The students are a major asset - especially if they're going to work in our schools when they've qualified. They're contributing a fresh view. I would imagine them being really very excited about this sort of teamwork.

The difference between understanding one another's point of view and actually taking it into account has to be recognised and resolved if collaboration is to progress. The identification of schools for participation in IT-INSET is a case in point. Hitherto, school of education tutors have made their individual choices without intervention by the Local Education Authority. Now, however, Brian Cruickshank argues:

> A good case could be made out, I think, for ringing the changes completely. I could see how IT-INSET could start from the very worst beginnings rather than from the best beginnings.

He regards some of the schools regularly involved in IT-INSET as the least in need, as 'tame institutions, fertile ground.' His view of the attributes required for participation in IT-INSET might worry some tutors:

> The key to it all has to be a willingness to work together. You find that willingness in many of the most able teachers -

whatever you mean by that - and many of the least able. Willingness to share has to be the starting point surely, then it doesn't matter whether they're good, bad or indifferent teachers - they're learning, and that's what it's all about. To think otherwise is to miss the point entirely.

The complexities of collaboration between a local education authority and a training institution begin to emerge.

Evaluation

Evaluation is now a paramount issue for local education authorities and concerns IT-INSET no less than all other in-service provision. Hitherto, it has been relatively informal. Now, however:

We could start asking the teachers to tell us. We perhaps just do not know enough about IT-INSET as it's practised. If there's anything we could do more of, it would be to find out a lot more and get more support on paper - to get more support for the basic ideas, to get more support for what it is the teachers really feel that they and the children are getting out of it. We haven't got enough data from the children. We've got some, perhaps, but not enough. We've got some from all over the country, but we could do with more from schools in Leicestershire. We could build up some evidence from local practice and use that to bang the drum in discussion with other groups who, instead of involving youngsters in INSET, are spending their time threshing around as a group of teachers on some particular thing - obviously with some eye to their pupils, but without really involving them in the exercise.

Clearly, more systematic evaluation of IT-INSET in Leicestershire will be inextricably linked to its future development.

Development

When IT-INSET begins to 'take' in a local education authority, the training institution is confronted with implications which extend far beyond offering INSET along with an initial training programme.

Progress in collaboration begins to shift the arena and multiply the tasks:

> We could bring in the professional tutors. They are becoming more and more pivotal. It may well be that, as a body, they don't know very much about IT-INSET. So we could encourage them to find out more about it and get them to locate it within their INSET policies for the whole school. We need more people doing more. Next Spring Term we could hold more meetings about IT-INSET. Throughout the last few years we've never, as an Authority, got together with those groups of teachers who've been involved, and we could do that through the professional tutors. There's an enormous amount that we could do; it's a question of getting down to the business. That's the whole problem, isn't it? The whole process of getting it on the agenda, making the time and the space in the Spring Term to do that. I could see the use of a secondment to do the groundwork, to organise meetings, prepare the papers, run the meetings. There's a very substantial body of work needed to draw the threads together, to define what to do next, what links to make with the advisers. And all of that means legwork. I'm just immediately thinking of ways in which that could be done. There's a line in the budget now which says IT-INSET, £12,000, and it's increased annually to take account of inflation. There's no reason why it should stay at £12,000. At one fell stroke it could be totally lost - or it could be enhanced. For it to be enhanced, we'd need to raise the advisory service's awareness of its benefits. IT-INSET would need to have a higher profile, but it would still be competing with other requests and priorities. However, if it were to be enhanced to the tune of, say, £4,000 or £5,000, it could pay for a secondment. In terms of the overall INSET budget, it's very small money. One way of going about it would be to get it on to the agenda, and get it agreed as broad authority policy. One can think of a strategy whereby that could be achieved. We have an INSET Working Group - an INSET Committee which includes politicians - and an INSET Advisory Committee of the professional associations. Both of those would have to be involved in supporting this. We've not actually taken any report to the professional INSET Advisory Committee. I can suddenly see a number of threads coming together if that

Committee discusses IT-INSET, so it's on the professional associations' agenda, it's in their minds. That's the way development happens in a local authority. That could be a seed to be sown in a number of professional asssociations up and down the country. Then, if you nurture it a little bit over the next year or so, it could bear enormous dividends. You can give them a job to do: 'We think this is important, but we're not sure. Can you help us? We'd like to know from your members.' Suddenly the evaluative aspect of IT-INSET, the classroom evaluation, could actually take off. The Department of Education and Science are now insisting on monitoring and evaluating INSET - it's a national preoccupation. The links with IT-INSET are obvious and yet the chances are that people like me in local authorities who've been involved in IT-INSET simply haven't made the connection.

The trend of this last contribution is significant. Brian Cruickshank had sat down for an unprecedented two hours to record his thoughts about IT-INSET for the purposes of this case study. That so much emerged in the way of new thinking underlines the overwhelming impediment to collaboration between local education authorities and training institutions - the lack of time to talk:

You have to be forced to sit down and think about it on an occasion like this. It's obvious we should be talking to the professional INSET Advisory Committee about it. I've put on the agenda of the next meeting the report of monitoring and evaluation of INSET for the Department of Education and Science. Why haven't I tied it in with IT-INSET? Because I haven't made the connection, or I haven't actually thought it through. It's taken the flash of a second to think of it, but there are always other pressing urgent things to do, 'phone calls to make. That's the reality. It is simply a matter of creating the time to think it through, to develop a strategy, to talk to colleagues who are going to be involved in working it. It's as simple and as complex as that. We've circulated papers, and Tony Gelsthorpe's report went to all advisers. We haven't had meetings; there's absolutely no reason why that shouldn't happen except that advisers' diaries are jam-packed. We need to create time and space, in the same way we've created space this morning, just to think a few things through. Things do emerge then as real ways forward.

Postscript

There is a kind of vigour about the collaboration between Leicestershire and Leicester University School of Education. It has a bedrock of shared commitment to the view that teacher education is about meeting the needs of children through meeting the needs of teachers and intending teachers. There is an open climate in which communication, if quantitatively inadequate, at least employs the same language. Issues remain, as they do for all local education authority/training institution collaborators, of turning goodwill into action, resolving differences in perspective, sharing practical tasks, and finding time.

Notes

1. TRIST stands for TVEI-Related In-Service Training, i.e. INSET funded by Government to support the Technical and Vocational Education Initiative.

2. Professional tutor posts were created in all Leicestershire secondary schools from 1987. Their job descriptions include responsibility for co-ordination of school-based INSET.

3. Curriculum review refers to a Leicestershire requirement that all schools review annually their curriculum principles and practice.

4. Tony Gelsthorpe is a headteacher who was seconded for one term to evaluate IT-INSET (Gelsthorpe 1986).

Part II
The national evaluation

This second part of the book is concerned with the national evaluation of IT-INSET conducted during 1986-87. In addition to assessing the value of IT-INSET to all those involved, the prime intention of the evaluation was to identify means by which the practice of IT-INSET may be progressively improved to the greater benefit of participants.

Chapter 8 describes the evolution of the evaluation strategy and the difficulties encountered in carrying it out, as well as setting out the instruments that were used. The formal evaluation instruments were complemented by the work of nine teachers, each seconded by their local education authorities for a term to evaluate IT-INSET in their own areas. None had undertaken an evaluation of this kind previously, but all brought a great deal of professional skill and experience to the task. Extracts from their reports are extensively used throughout Part II to illustrate points and to add the flavour of IT-INSET in practice to the statistical data. This sharing of the evaluative task has been a further demonstration that expertise is not anyone's exclusive prerogative and that bringing together different perspectives can enhance everyone's learning.

The quality of IT-INSET practice in 1986-87 is examined in Chapter 9. A particularly useful outcome is the confirmation that IT-INSET is not simply 'done' or 'not done', but is undertaken at distinctively different levels of effectiveness. The characteristics of each level illuminate the action that can be taken by participants to enhance the quality of their own programmes.

Chapter 10 summarises the benefits of IT-INSET for each category of participants - pupils, students, teachers, tutors, schools, training institutions and local education authorities.

The evaluation revealed that the training institution was the single greatest influence on the quality of IT-INSET practice. Chapter 11 analyses the key differences between more and less successful institutions in terms of a number of factors which helped and hindered effective practice by their teams.

But there were other influences on the quality of IT-INSET practice also, and the final chapter in Part II examines helping and hindering factors arising from the influences of tutors, headteachers and the teams themselves.

8

The evaluation strategy

Engaging in evaluation of the curriculum is a key principle of IT-INSET (see p. 9) and IT-INSET itself develops certain evaluation skills among participants. These are the skills involved in monitoring what children are actually doing and making judgements about what they are learning and its worthwhileness. They are associated with systematic observation, analysis of evidence, making theories explicit, and using the resulting perspectives and conclusions to improve children's subsequent learning.

In one sense, this evaluation which is embedded in the doing of IT-INSET should be distinguished from the evaluation of the IT-INSET process itself. Although the evaluation of children's learning makes an essential contribution, evaluation of the IT-INSET process also involves gathering evidence at school, training institution and local education authority levels, as well as at the levels of individual participants, teams and classes of children. It requires using as many means of information gathering as possible and, in consequence, it necessitates involvement of people other than team participants.

At the same time, some current thinking about evaluation related to in-service training, such as the work done on TRIST evaluation (Holly *et al.* 1987) attaches as much importance to evaluation *as* INSET as it does to evaluation *of* INSET. In other words, just as the participants in IT-INSET teams can learn one set of evaluation skills, those involved in evaluation of IT-INSET can learn a different, if overlapping, set of skills through their work. In devising a strategy for the evaluation of IT-INSET nationally, therefore, the first priority was to consider both kinds of participants in the evaluation process and ensure that they would indeed acquire useful skills as a consequence of the way they contributed to doing or evaluating IT-INSET.

The collaborative principle inherent in IT-INSET is crucial to its evaluation, since it is through collaboration and the sharing of perceptions that participants' learning is enhanced. There are several implications of this. First, any external evaluator - one who is not a participant in an IT-INSET team - should find ways of working alongside teams in order to share their perceptions of a common experience. Second, teachers, tutors and students must see their evaluation role as extending beyond reflection on their own particular experience. This means considering the benefits to others in their teams, as well as to the wider constituencies of the school, training institution and local education authority. Third, it means that communication links between the different participants need to be fully used, so that maximum use is made of the evidence available.

All this is crucial because, while improving children's learning remains the ultimate goal and benchmark against which IT-INSET needs to be judged, trying to evaluate IT-INSET by assessing impact on children alone would be extremely difficult if not impossible. The reasons for this have been touched on by the Department of Education and Science in a note on *Monitoring and Evaluation* (DES 1987a) and are discussed further below. Thus, though evaluation of children's learning by IT-INSET teams makes an essential contribution to the overall evaluation of IT-INSET, it is also necessary to consider 'intermediate measures' such as those related to impact on teachers, tutors and students. These, as the *Monitoring and Evaluation* note points out, must provide much if not all the information relevant to this kind of evaluation.

The difficulties of IT-INSET evaluation are exacerbated by the wide age range of pupils and wide subject spectrum involved, and by the need to be concerned with evaluation at individual, team, school, training institution, and local education authority levels. Reconciling the diverse and sometimes conflicting needs and concerns in the focus of an evaluation is virtually impossible. The chosen strategy for the national evaluation was therefore to collect information from a broad range of individual participants, teams, schools, training institutions, local education authorities, seconded teachers and external evaluators, to collate and analyse this information, and to interpret the findings in ways which would be relevant to teams, schools, training institutions and local education authorities.

In summary, the key principles underlying the national evaluation of IT-INSET were:

- participation in evaluation as part of a learning process;
- collaboration with others to extend the range of available perspectives;
- focus on the perceived benefits to those involved and to their schools, training institutions and local education authorities;
- effective interpretation and communication of outcomes by and between all those participating in evaluation throughout the IT-INSET network; as a means to
- maximum utilisation of evidence and the continuation of IT-INSET evaluation after the completion of the national evaluation.

The evolution of the strategy

To describe the national evaluation of IT-INSET as if it were planned in detail in advance would be misleading. As with many similar evaluations, the design emerged gradually and was influenced by data already gathered as well as by changes in circumstances. One of the earlier documents describing the strategy set out the plans as follows:

One important consideration is that the foci eventually chosen are seen by participants to be important and valuable areas of enquiry. ... The most attractive rationale for evaluation is ... the use of the six principles [of IT-INSET] as the method, as well as the focus of evaluation. This would mean that:

1. The evaluation would concern itself with observing and analysing team practice;
2. It would seek to make sense of what is happening by setting it in the context of relevant theories;
3. It would seek to reconsider the value of the IT-INSET process as a vehicle for professional reflection and training, and re-assess priorities within the goals set;
4. It would aim to develop and improve the IT-INSET 'curriculum process' to improve the effectiveness of the team's classroom experience, with the goal of consolidating effective practice beyond 1987;
5. It would involve the evaluator(s) working as a team and as part of existing teams, in order to capitalise on the range of knowledge, experience and insights available, particularly at the stage of planning the evaluation;

6. It would aim to involve other people in a collaborative process of evaluation, both during [1985/87] and beyond.

(Peacock 1985)

It was apparent that a range of ways of gathering information would be needed, and at this early stage the techniques advocated were case studies undertaken by staff of the Centre for Evaluation and Development in Teacher Education and others, audio/video recording of teams in operation on a first session/last session basis, follow-up of participants after their involvement in IT-INSET teams, self-reporting by individuals, teams and co-ordinators based on their own evaluation priorities, and questionnaires based on critical indicators of effective IT-INSET practice.

These proposals led to joint evaluation plans being developed between the Centre and a number of the most committed training institutions to evaluate IT-INSET programmes operating in the academic year 1985/86. Each of these was a unique blend of training institution and Centre concerns. For example, one college wished to focus on the cost-benefit aspects of IT-INSET, and it was agreed that the college would undertake a cost analysis of its IT-INSET programme, while the Centre evaluator would study benefits to students and tutors, and a seconded headteacher would investigate the benefits to teachers, schools and the local education authority. Reports of all of these studies were subsequently circulated by the Centre (Goulden 1986; Peacock 1986; Brooke 1986).

From studies like these, undertaken in a number of areas of the country, it was intended that common concerns, and thus common criteria for a national evaluation strategy to be implemented in 1986/87, would emerge. However, 1985/86 was a year in which financial crises in higher education and teachers' industrial action seriously affected several programmes, and inevitably it was involvement in evaluation, rather than involvement in IT-INSET itself, which suffered. Thus the collaborative programmes worked out with a number of training institutions were never completed, and the strategy for the 1986/87 evaluation had to be based on the outcomes of only four evaluation studies of practice at local level.

During this period, however, two different ways of developing critical indicators of effective practice were devised and piloted, and one of these - the team questionnaire - was subsequently modified and used in the final study. It also became apparent that some of the proposed techniques would not be practicable in a systematic and widespread form, namely the audio/video recording and the follow-up of students' and teachers' performance after their IT-INSET experience. Both of these techniques were used to some extent, and a good deal of circumstantial evidence about participants' subsequent performance did accumulate, but it became obvious that the resources available would not permit them to be used on an extensive scale as ways of obtaining evidence.

By early 1986 the plan for the national evaluation had developed into what was described as a 'figure and ground' strategy, which was to involve the following.

1. The systematic gathering of background evidence nationally, using centrally designed questionnaires, evaluation records and analysis of documents.
2. The use of case study methods for gathering detailed evidence about a given school, team or individual, by a variety of methods, some being based on agreed formats, others being unique to a particular context.
3. The co-ordination of case-study work by meetings between CEDTE staff and those undertaking local data-gathering, such as seconded teachers, headteachers, college co-ordinators, etc.
4. The use of a range of techniques for gathering information, as a means of corroborating evidence and generating further questions, as well as to avoid dependence on single sources.
5. A progressive evolution or definition of IT-INSET evaluation methods which are appropriate for [training] institutions and [local education authorities] to carry out themselves.

(CEDTE 1986)

Constraints on the evaluation strategy

The major constraints were of a practical nature, arising out of the dimensions of the IT-INSET programmes on the one hand and the resources and evidence available on the other. The most significant of these were as follows.

Substantive differences Children aged 3 to 16 were involved, and students ranged from first year BEd to post-graduate certificate in education. The focus or curriculum issue chosen by teams covered almost every subject and many organisational aspects of classroom life, and encompassed both broad and narrow topics.

Geographical distribution of IT-INSET programmes
Twenty-one training institutions were operating IT-INSET programmes at the time of the national evaluation, located as far apart as Devon and Cumbria, with some concentration in the Midlands and the North. The main difficulty created by this was the cost, in time and resources, of visiting programmes to observe IT-INSET in action.

Stages of development of programmes Experience of operating IT-INSET varied from training institutions undertaking small pilot schemes for the first time to those organising extensive programmes in more than one year of their BEd course, perhaps for the sixth successive year, with backing from their local education authorities.

Timing of programmes Programmes operated in autumn, spring or summer terms, mainly for a single term but in some cases for two terms. That they were intermittent and on a specific day each week meant that extensive study of any given programme by an individual was difficult. Time spent by teams in school also varied from as little as two hours to as much as one day per week.

The technical difficulties of measuring pupils' learning
There are no validated instruments capable of measuring changes in learning across the entire age and subject spectrum involved in IT-INSET, particularly since impact may take a long time and not be readily observable. There would, in any case, be massive problems in attempting to relate changes, even where conclusive, to an intermittent experience which is only one among many other variables.

Staffing available to the evaluation During the period of the national evaluation from 1985 to 1987, only one person was available full-time to evaluate IT-INSET. Two of the other staff of the Centre for Evaluation and Development in Teacher Education had responsibilities other than IT-INSET, and all three were responsible for carrying out development and dissemination functions in parallel with evaluation activity. However, some additional human resources were available to contribute to the evaluation. Prior to April 1987, poolable fellowships were available to the Centre for work on school-focused INSET, and during 1986/87 most of these were utilised to second teachers with experience of IT-INSET to assist with evaluation in their local education authorities. Co-ordinators of IT-INSET in training institutions and in some cases advisers also saw it as part of their role to assist with evaluation, although the time they had available was sometimes very limited.

The nature of the evidence available

The national evaluation relied to a great extent on the self-perceptions of participants for two reasons. First was the assumption that, if IT-INSET as a novel approach to teacher education can be improved through evaluation, then the focus of study needed to be on the process and its benefits as perceived by the participants themselves - children, students, teachers, tutors, schools, training institutions, and local education authorities. As Marsh (1986) has pointed out, in analysing the perceptions of all these participants, questions of philosophy, pedagogy, organisation and resources have to be addressed. Secondly, many of the constraints enumerated above necessitated reliance on such self-reported perceptions.

Many difficulties exist in gaining access to the cognitions of teachers and others involved. Koziol and Burns (1986), for instance, have shown that teachers' self-reports are often unreliable, but that they can be accurate if certain procedures are used systematically, such as focused inventories. Halkes (1986) has echoed what many earlier researchers have suggested in advising that several complementary methods of gathering evidence should be used, in order to counterbalance implicit influences and to cross-check data. However, Smyth (1984) rejects the notion implied in some such studies that teachers are not experts in self-monitoring, provided that the potential for action is allied to engagement in reflection.

Co-ordinating the efforts of seconded teachers working in different contexts over a wide geographical area at different times also presented major problems of standardisation of data collection. Strict comparability of evidence from these sources was therefore difficult to achieve. However, a wide range of reports based on first-hand observation by the staff of the Centre for Evaluation and Development in Teacher Education, team members, co-ordinators, and others had been accumulating over the six years since the previous evaluation and, while mostly unsystematic and subjective in style, these provided valuable circumstantial background information.

Finally, systematic evidence collected in the 1981 evaluation (Ashton *et al.* 1983), along with the instruments used for obtaining this evidence, were available for replication and comparison.

Evaluation instruments and techniques

Several instruments were designed to collect background information from a wide range of participants in all IT-INSET programmes operating during the academic year 1986/87.

1. The replication of *questionnaires used in the 1981 evaluation* to obtain evidence from chief education officers (Appendix 2), training institution principals/directors (Appendix 3) and headteachers (Appendix 4) of their perceptions of the benefits of IT-INSET to their particular authority/institution/school.

2. A *team questionnaire* to establish in detail how teams actually operated in practice, which included items designed as disqualifiers to establish the extent of conformity with established IT-INSET principles and processes (Appendix 5).

3. An evaluation workbook consisting of:

- a *structured diary* through which individual participants could keep records of their work and achievement throughout the IT-INSET programme (Appendix 6);
- a *relative benefits questionnaire* to establish, at the end of a programme, how individuals perceived the benefits of IT-INSET in relation to other aspects of their experience (Appendix 7).

Additional background information was available from two other sources:

- observation by staff of the Centre for Evaluation and Development in Teacher Education of IT-INSET programmes in all training institutions operating during the year;
- the proceedings of three national conferences which were held during the academic year 1986/87 - *IT-INSET and subject studies, Planning and preparation for IT-INSET* (CEDTE 1987), and *Learning to evaluate IT-INSET*.

Case studies were undertaken by seconded staff from eight local education authorities - Birmingham, Dudley, Essex, Lancashire, Leeds, Leicestershire (two), Oxfordshire, and West Sussex. Each secondment was for one term, although in some cases the period was extended so that the secondee could undertake further evaluation and/or dissemination on behalf of the authority.

The common elements of the case studies were:

- focusing on benefits for teachers, tutors, schools, and local education authorities;
- contrasting the expectations of participants with their perceptions of the outcomes;
- interviewing participants using jointly agreed schedules;
- observing the full IT-INSET cycle for a particular team on a particular day, especially the discussion phase;
- looking for helping and hindering factors, in relation to such issues as communication, planning and preparation, organisation, teamwork, and ways of reporting;
- identifying ways in which headteachers facilitated IT-INSET.

In addition, for a few selected teams, the authors of case studies were involved in:

- observing classes at non-IT-INSET times;
- seeking evidence/indicators of benefits to children;
- comparing team records with their own records.

Seconded teachers tended not to quantify their data. Categorising discursive material from interviews and questionnaires is a formidable task, and their time was limited. They preferred in most cases to exercise their judgement of the trends emerging from the data, and represented these either as syntheses or by extensive quotations of participants' comments.

A note on the seconded teachers

Those involved were primary teachers and headteachers, as well as one deputy headteacher and one head of department from secondary schools. Some, but not all, had experienced IT-INSET previously. Prior to their work locally, they met together with those responsible for the national evaluation to discuss priorities and agree a common agenda of concerns on which to focus collection of evidence.

Their initial concerns were with observing, interviewing and writing: most felt themselves to be very inexperienced in these 'research' skills. The preliminary meetings sought to give them support and to help them to be clearer about what they were looking for.

What did they do? Most spent the bulk of their one-term secondments in schools observing IT-INSET in practice. Some were also able to be in schools at times other than when IT-INSET was taking place, providing valuable opportunities for comparison and discussion. All carried out extensive interviews with team members, headteachers, and training institution and local education authority staff. All met as a group and with staff of the Centre for Evaluation and Development in Teacher Education at least twice during their secondments.

What did they learn? Some of the skills developed were those also learned by IT-INSET participants, such as clarifying issues about learning, identifying evidence of learning or its absence and linking this to observed teaching strategies, analysing evidence from observations, drawing provisional conclusions and checking these against further observations, and planning their work of information-gathering in ways that enabled them to answer questions they had raised.

There was also a good deal of learning of what might be described as 'research skills'. Most soon came to enjoy interviewing and some reflected afterwards on the inadequacy of their interviewing schedules, suggesting numerous ways in which they could be improved. The quotations from their reports in the chapters which follow show their ability to illuminate situations and to communicate insights, though several struggled initially with the skills of writing in a new genre and one or two did not fully master them.

Some of their learning also involved them developing their existing skills as managers but in a new context. For example, they were encountering many new people in situations which required them to establish productive working relationships, and they were taking account of various new perspectives on their own roles. In addition, they learned new INSET roles, as disseminators of practice or as focal points in a developing IT-INSET network. In most cases, their local education authorities saw the benefits of using them in these ways.

These secondments have thus provided a variety of benefits to the teachers concerned and to the INSET systems in which they work.

Summary

The evidence on which the national evaluation of IT-INSET was based can be characterised by the following.

1. Systematic and quantifiable evidence about how teams operated collected by means of the team questionnaire, and about the relative benefits of IT-INSET using the relative benefits questionnaire.
2. Individuals' descriptions of their activities collected, categorised and quantified through the evaluation workbooks.
3. Perceptions of benefit at school, training institution and local education authority levels collected and categorised through the questionnaires to headteachers, directors/principals and chief education officers.
4. Evidence relating to the process and benefits of IT-INSET from the observations of staff of the Centre for Evaluation and Development in Teacher Education and seconded teachers, from the proceedings of conferences, meetings and seminars, and by utilisation of the communications network created among IT-INSET institutions.

9
IT-INSET in practice

This chapter provides data from a number of sources indicating how members of teams engaged in IT-INSET. The first source of data, the national evaluation workbooks (Appendix 6), referred to for brevity as 'diaries', contain team members' weekly records of their activities. These records provide evidence of the extent to which participants observed and analysed practice and are categorised according to the level of skill revealed: four skill levels are identified. Team questionnaire responses are then analysed to determine teams' perceptions of their achievements in the skills related to each of the six principles of IT-INSET (see p. 9). These data are supplemented by the assessments of seconded teachers who observed teams at work. Finally, the team questionnaires are analysed for indications of practice inconsistent with IT-INSET.

What did team members actually do?

Team members were asked to keep a diary throughout the programme, making their entries under four headings:

• Major action planned/taken to find out more about what the children are learning
• Major questions raised
• Reading done, resources used, others consulted
• Contacts made with Headteacher or other staff.

An initial analysis of entries under the latter two headings showed no significant relationship with other characteristics of teams. Entries under the first two headings were categorised as in Table 9.1.

116

Table 9.1   The categorisation of diary entries

Diary instruction	*Category name*	*Examples*
Major action planned/ taken to find out more about what the children were learning	Did	All of the entries which indicated what the team, or the individual member, had done with the children. These entries were effectively brief lesson plans. While it may have been that the teaching had been devised with a diagnostic purpose, it was not credited with that intention unless it was made explicit.
	Observation	All references to the deployment of team members as observers, or to observation strategies, or to targets for observation.
	Assessment	Any references to testing or to teaching strategies explicitly designed to reveal pupils' capabilities.
Major questions/issues raised	Teaching	Teaching questions concerned with the action that the team should take in future work with the children. These questions implied that the pupils' responses, behaviour or learning were not at issue, but that decisions needed to be taken about how the teaching should be carried out. For example:
		How can we improve teacher questioning?

/cont.

Diary instruction	Category name	Examples
	Learning	How much input should we have given, i.e. should we let the children carry out the process themselves or should we push them in certain directions? Should children be grouped by age or ability? Learning questions reflected interest in the pupils' responses, behaviour or learning. For example: We wondered if the task has been too constricting so the children hadn't the experiences to call upon to make the boat. Why was the play on the table so much more concentrated and intense - was it because both participants at the table happened to be girls?
	IT-INSET process	IT-INSET process questions most often concerned observation and evaluation, but also included reflections on teamwork and contacts with other members of the school's staff. For example: Should we be looking at achievement and not ability? What were the benefits for the pupils, members of the team, the institution?

Given the varying lengths of programmes, only the first and the last two weeks were taken into account in analysing 247 diaries. The entries were distributed as shown in Table 9.2.

Table 9.2   Distribution of diary entries between categories

Type of entry	First two weeks		Last two weeks	
	No.	%	No.	%
Action planned:				
Teaching	215	87	220	89
Observing	156	63	91	37
Assessing	31	13	37	15
Major questions raised about:				
Teaching	153	62	132	53
Pupils' learning	164	66	127	51
Observing and evaluating	82	33	65	26

These entries were used as evidence of the levels at which team members had observed and analysed practice. The concept of four levels of IT-INSET practice was first developed in the 1981 evaluation (Ashton *et al.* 1983). They can be described in the following terms.

Level 0: No evidence of IT-INSET skills of observing and analysing practice. The characteristics of Level 0 are that no observation is reported and, therefore, no analysis. The team is effectively an unreflective teaching group.

Level 1: Doing IT-INSET activities without apparent understanding. The characteristics of Level 1 are that team members report making observations but make no analyses of them and raise no questions about what they have seen. Thus they do not appear to understand the purpose of observing.

Level 2: Conceptualising IT-INSET skills of observing and analysing practice. The characteristics of Level 2 are that team members make observations, appear to understand the purpose of doing so, make analyses, and raise questions about what they have seen.

Level 3: Applying IT-INSET skills of observing and analysing practice. The characteristics of Level 3 are that team members appear to have acquired the skills of observing and analysing practice with understanding to the extent that they are applying them purposefully to the study and improvement of pupils' learning.

Table 9.3 shows the distribution of the 247 team members whose diaries were analysed between the four levels of IT-INSET practice. That as many as 59 per cent of team members were operating at Level 3 is indicative of the considerable progress made in the implementation of IT-INSET since the 1981 evaluation, when only about one team member in eight was reaching this level (Ashton *et al.* 1983).

Table 9.3 Distribution of team members between the four levels of IT-INSET practice.

Level	Number	Percentage
0	19	8
1	33	13
2	49	20
3	146	59
Total	247	100

Achievements in relation to the six principles

Team members were asked by means of a questionnaire (Appendix 5) to describe their activities and to assess their achievements in respect of all six skill areas of IT-INSET:

1. observing practice;
2. analysing practice and applying theory;

3. evaluating the curriculum;
4. developing the curriculum;
5. working as a team; and
6. involving the school's other teachers in the process.

Table 9.4 gives the responses of 187 teams to a question inviting them to indicate the extent to which they felt they had put each of the six principles into practice.

Table 9.4   Teams' views on the extent to which they had practised the six principles

Principles	Percentage of teams rating themselves as having achieved:		
	Fully	*Partly*	*Not at all*
Observing practice	29	63	8
Analysing practice and applying theory	19	73	8
Working as a team	68	26	5
Evaluating the curriculum	15	61	24
Developing the curriculum	27	57	17
Involving others in the process	20	52	27

All but a small minority of teams thought that they had been at least partly successful in observing practice, analysing practice and applying theory, and working as a team. This accords with the evidence of the diaries. Two-thirds of teams thought that their teamwork had been entirely successful and one-third that their observation and analysis of practice had been entirely successful. Fewer teams thought that they had been successful in evaluating and developing the curriculum and in involving other teachers in their work. Around a quarter thought that they had achieved nothing in these three areas.

Table 9.5 shows the results of carrying out a principal components analysis on these ratings of achievement. Factor 1 can be interpreted as a 'general achievement' factor, encompassing perceptions of achievement on all six scales, while Factor 2 distinguishes three particular aspects of achievement as being related to each other, namely observing classroom practice, analysing practice and applying theory, and working as a team. These may best be described as lower-level, practical attributes of the IT-INSET process, as distinct from the other three attributes which follow on from success at the lower level. Factor 2 can therefore be described as a 'basic processes' factor.

Table 9.5   Loadings of ratings of achievement on two factors*

Principles	Factor 1	Factor 2
Observing classroom practice	0.765	0.772
Analysing practice and applying theory	0.538	0.367
Evaluating the curriculum	0.762	-0.247
Developing the curriculum	0.722	-0.505
Working as a team	0.658	0.171
Involving others in the process	0.536	-0.140

* Factor 1 accounts for 38% of the variance and Factor 2 for 18.2%.

Thus the skill areas appear to be linked in two groups. Observing practice, analysing practice and applying theory, and teamwork appear to be related so that teams rating themselves highly on one tend to rate themselves highly on the other. The smaller number of teams who rate highly their achievements in evaluating and developing the curriculum and involving other teachers tend to rate themselves highly across the board. This suggests that teams perceive themselves as generally successful in all areas of IT-INSET, including the more advanced skill areas, or as successful only in the lower-level areas, or as generally unsuccessful.

This self-perception of levels of achievement accords with evidence from other sources. The following extracts from reports by three teachers who were seconded as IT-INSET evaluators are typical.

Seconded teacher's observation of programmes in progress and interviews with twenty-eight class teachers associated with Training Institutions 01 and 25:

Observing classroom practice All teams recognised the need for an observer. The depth or quality of observation varied greatly but certainly all teams considered what the children were actually doing. It was the how and why that might not be noted.

Analysing practice and applying theory Class teachers of all teams felt they had analysed practice quite naturally, particularly in drawing upon remarks made by the observer and comments of fellow team members involved in the teaching sessions.
Teachers were a little uncertain about their application of theory. In most cases they felt the tutor provided the theory or suggested direction towards it for other team members to pick up. A lot depended upon levels of discussion. Where lively, open conversation arose from the observer's notes or team members' experiences, then thoughts about applying theory would arise quite naturally.

Working as a team Certainly most teachers expressed a sense of having enjoyed the IT-INSET project. If the experience had not been a good one, they were nevertheless keen to do it again, feeling that next time they would be wiser. Undoubtedly, enjoyment was a product of good teamwork:

I enjoyed the rapport of working as a team.
It was a real treat.
A refreshingly realistic experience.
A most beneficial and worthwhile experience with everybody learning.
A great reassurance for teachers.

Many team members were slightly apprehensive about teaching in front of others, but confidence built up and respect between team members developed with the passage of time.

Evaluating the curriculum It was often quite difficult to establish whether the IT-INSET work reflected any rethinking of the school's curriculum.

Developing the curriculum Teachers seemed quite thrilled with the response of children to the range of skills and concepts introduced by the IT-INSET approach. For example: 'It's amazing what ground we've covered.' Teachers felt that the work attempted had reinforced their belief that written work is not always needed as evidence of progress.

Involving others in the process This was perhaps the most difficult aspect of IT-INSET.

Seconded teacher's observation of IT-INSET in progress in ten schools associated with Training Institution 02:

Observing classroom practice Most team members claimed to be observing constantly. Systematic observation, however, occurred only where teachers were aware of this element and where organisation allowed. Even so, there were no records kept and little use was made of these observations during the discussion time.

Analysing practice and applying theory Observations were only used when they illustrated issues raised by the team.

Working as a team Effective teamwork was more easily recognised in teams where members accepted their change in roles and where their attitudes were 'open' with all members accepting the role of learner. It was very difficult for tutors to play a full part in all aspects of the teams' work because of their workload.

Evaluating the curriculum The best example of this was during a discussion between three students and a teacher. The teacher demonstrated, in the class, her concern for the effectiveness of teaching. In the discussion she listened intently to the students and gently guided them to this focus by the use of questions and short statements of her own views. The worst example was when a tutor actually prevented this type of discussion from taking place.

Developing the curriculum No examples.

Involving other teachers No examples.

Twenty-seven visits by a seconded teacher to observe IT-INSET in eight schools associated with Training Institution 06:

Some *observation of classroom practice* was noticed on most of my visits. The *analysis of classroom practice* which followed the observation was also a noticeable part of many of the discussions, the purpose being to make sense of what had been observed in the classroom. However, the *application of theory* linked to the analysis of classroom practice was not as easy to pinpoint. I believe, however, that the students were able to make sense of their college-based theory and relate it to practice.

There was considerable evidence to show that those involved were *working as a team* to capitalise on a range of knowledge, enthusiasm, and experience. In some cases the team spirit took longer to manifest itself, possibly due to the fact that there were inadequate opportunities to discuss what had happened in the classroom. Sometimes individual personalities made team-building difficult initially.

The aim of *curriculum evaluation* is to reconsider the value of children's learning and consequently to reassess priorities. The question 'How worthwhile was it?' was often asked with reference to what the children actually did and actually learned. There was little evidence of *curriculum development* during the project but there were, I believe, clear indications that the project will lead to such development during the next school year.

The *involvement of other teachers in the process of collaborative curriculum review* was in most cases difficult or impracticable. There was some discussion of the IT-INSET philosophy in staffrooms, but little real evidence of the involvement of other teachers or that what was being taught and evaluated by the team was reaching other parts of the school. There were, however, indications that there may be spin-offs from the project during the next term, especially in schools where staff team-building and purposeful leadership go side by side.

These reports by seconded teachers confirm, on the whole, teams' own reports. Teams were seen to be achieving greater success in the areas of observing practice, analysing practice and applying theory, and working as a team than in evaluating and developing the curriculum and involving other teachers. It is also apparent from these reports, however, that teams associated with some training institutions were working at a generally higher level than were teams associated with others.

Practice inconsistent with IT-INSET

This apparent difference in level of IT-INSET practice between training institutions was confirmed by the analysis of evidence arising from the 'disqualifiers' included in the team questionnaire (Appendix 5). Ten such items were included (Table 9.6), to which affirmative answers indicated practices inconsistent with IT-INSET - for example, that no observation had been undertaken, that there had been no analysis of pupil learning, that less than fifteen minutes had been spent each week on evaluating the team's classroom work, or that the issue to be investigated had been determined by the training institution rather than by the school.

On this basis it appeared that about 23 per cent of teams, concentrated in four training institutions, had operated in ways that precluded or severely inhibited learning the intrinsic skills of IT-INSET. (The question of differences in level of operation between training institutions is discussed further in Chapter 11.)

Summary

IT-INSET may be construed as having operated at four levels, each successively higher level conferring increased benefits in terms both of team members learning the intrinsic skills of IT-INSET and of the learning of pupils. These benefits, to team members and pupils, are summarised in Table 9.7.

Table 9.6   List of disqualifiers

Disqualifier number	Disqualifying alternatives
D1	The headteacher was responsible for planning classroom work.
	The training institution co-ordinator was responsible for determining the topic.
	The tutor was responsible for determining the topic.
D2	None of the planning was undertaken by the team as a whole.
D3	Team members never taught the whole class.
D4	Team members never observed the whole class.
	Team members never observed a group of pupils.
	Team members never observed an individual pupil.
D5	Time spent on evaluation was less than 15 minutes.
	Time spent on team planning was less than 15 minutes.
D6	The team had no clear focus for its work in the last weeks of the programme.
D7	The team never discussed any of the principles of IT-INSET.
D8	Team members stuck to their traditional roles.
	The team was very hierarchical.
	Team members all had different purposes.
	Team members learned little from each other.
D9	Few team members contributed ideas.
	The team never analysed pupils' learning.
D10	A sub-group dominated team discussion during the last weeks of the programme.

Table 9.7　　　Benefits to team members and pupils associated with the four levels of IT-INSET practice

Level	Benefits
0 - Non-IT-INSET	*Team benefits:* generally only accruing from teachers, students and tutors working co-operatively in schools. *Pupil benefits:* extra adults in the classroom, short-term enrichment of experience.
1 - Doing IT-INSET	*Additional team benefits:* skills of teamwork. *Additional pupil benefits:* none.
2 - Conceptualising IT-INSET	*Additional team benefits:* skills of teamwork, observation and analysis of classroom practice and pupil learning. *Additional pupil benefits:* considered improvement in learning opportunities in the course of the programme.
3 - Applying IT-INSET	*Additional team benefits:* skills of evaluating and developing the curriculum collaboratively with colleagues. *Additional pupil benefits:* continuing improvement in the curriculum.

10

The benefits of IT-INSET

This chapter summarises data from the national evaluation describing the benefits of IT-INSET as perceived by the various participants and others. First, the benefits to pupils are reported. Then the benefits to each group of team members - students, teachers and tutors - are considered. Finally, benefits to schools, training institutions and local education authorities are summarised, as perceived by headteachers, principals/directors of training institutions, and chief education officers respectively.

Benefits to pupils

Team members - teachers, students and tutors - maintained diaries (Appendix 6) throughout their IT-INSET programmes, which included pre- and post-assessments of their pupils' learning in the curriculum area in which their team was working. Analysis of 247 of these diaries provided evidence of pupils' learning gains as perceived by team members. Table 10.1 shows the number and percentage of team members reporting learning gains in two categories:

1. general - children had covered more work, increased achievements generally;
2. specific - children had gained named concepts and/or skills.

It can be seen that the great majority of team members (95 per cent) identified specific improvements in pupils' achievements, with a significant proportion (40 per cent) identifying gains of a more general kind.

These data can be supplemented by a quotation from one of the seconded teachers, part of whose evaluation in schools associated with Training Institution 06 involved interviewing children:

On my visits to schools, I was able to ascertain the views of the children as they worked on the tasks set them by the team. They all seemed to enjoy the extra attention they were receiving, and gave the impression that they 'liked all the teachers'. One child expressed the view that, 'You could get on with them'. Other comments included: 'It's exciting', 'It has taught us a lot but we didn't have to write it down', 'I liked the practical work', 'It was a help for our new school - meeting new teachers', 'It was good fun', 'It's better than other work'. The only negative view expressed centred around the fact that the project in one school was on Thursday afternoons: 'We missed games,' was the unanimous view. The children's parents were, I was informed by the children, also very interested and impressed. 'My Mum thinks it's a really good idea,' was a typical comment.

Table 10.1   Team members' assessments of gains in pupil learning

Nature of learning gains	Number of team members reporting gains	Percentage of team members reporting gains
General	96	40
Specific	225	95

In assessing the benefits of IT-INSET to their schools, 37 per cent of headteachers made a particularly strong point of the gains they had perceived for pupils. These gains included improved standards, increased individual attention, increased experience of group work, improved oral skills, and exposure to new ideas, resources and experiences. In the course of interviews, also, heads and class teachers reported a wide range of benefits to pupils and emphasised the value of increased adult attention, with consequent effects on work standards, additional stimulation and interest, and the pupils' enjoyment of IT-INSET. Children endorsed these perceptions. One of the seconded teachers identified the benefits to pupils shown in Table 10.2 from analysis of interviews with fourteen heads and fifteen class teachers (Training Institution 04).

Table 10.2   Benefits to pupils

Benefit	No. of mentions
Relating to new people	17
Working in small groups	16
More individual attention and extra help	12
Doing more and different work	12
New ideas and approaches	9
Curriculum review and development	8
Greater input of people, expertise and resources	6
Increased stimulus and motivation	4
Personal development	2
Enjoyment	2
Areas of difficulty pinpointed	1
Development of closer relationships	1

Students' perceptions of benefit

The relative benefits questionnaire (Appendix 7) asked students to 'Rate each of the aspects of your college course on a scale from 1 (of no benefit whatsoever) to 6 (of maximum benefit) in terms of *how they helped you as a teacher to cater appropriately for children's learning*.' Table 10.3, which gives the mean ratings for the 181 students who responded, shows that students rated IT-INSET the second most beneficial element in their initial training course.

Students listed the benefits of IT-INSET, compared with block teaching practice, as providing:

• better opportunities to observe both pupils and other people teaching;

- a greater range of ideas and information *via* other team members;
- more constructive and supportive professional relationships;
- more feedback on performance;
- more preparation time;
- enhanced opportunities for reflection and discussion;
- less unhelpful stress.

Students saw the benefits of block teaching practice, compared with IT-INSET, as providing:

- more realistic experience;
- greater opportunities for teaching;
- greater responsibility for managing classes and the curriculum;
- greater continuity, and hence better opportunities to become familiar with the pupils and their learning and to form good working relationships with teachers and schools.

Table 10.3   Students' perceptions of the relative benefits of IT-INSET

Aspect of course	Mean rating
Block teaching practice	5.57
IT-INSET	4.74
College-based work with children	4.30
Observation in schools	4.09
Curriculum content and method	3.98
Theories of teaching and learning	3.71
Private study	3.40
Main academic subjects	3.34

An additional perspective was provided by a questionnaire administered by one of the seconded teachers to sixty-five students from Training Institution 05. The benefits reported were:

- the development of teamwork and co-operative skills;
- a growth in confidence about their teaching ability, especially in areas which were not their specialisms;

- seeing experienced teachers at work;
- observation and evaluation of how children learn;
- the development of organisational skills.

In summary, students perceive block teaching practice as a simulation of teaching, their ultimate goal and preferred activity, whereas they view IT-INSET as a preparation for teaching and, as such, as the second most useful element in their courses.

Teachers' perceptions of benefit

Teachers were asked to 'Rate each of the forms of in-service experience on a scale from 1 (of no benefit whatsoever) to 6 (of maximum benefit) in terms of *how they helped you as a teacher to cater appropriately for children's learning*.'

Table 10.4 gives the mean ratings for the seventy-six respondents and shows that teachers considered residential short courses and full-time secondments, in that order, as the most beneficial forms of INSET. IT-INSET was rated most highly of all other types of INSET.

Table 10.4   Teachers' ratings of different forms of INSET

Forms of INSET	Mean rating
Residential short courses	4.92
Full-time secondment	4.80
IT-INSET	4.76
INSET run by teachers themselves	4.62
Day courses with cover	4.32
Part-time extended courses	4.29
INSET organised by outside agency	4.12
After school courses/meetings	3.28

An analysis of interviews of 144 class teachers conducted by six of the seconded teachers summarised the benefits they perceived as:

- opportunity to work with small groups of children;
- new ideas;
- opportunity to observe children and evaluate learning;
- teamwork/collaboration;
- links with the college;
- opportunity to observe others teaching;
- builds confidence, encourages reflection on teaching;
- opportunity to discuss/exchange ideas/explain ideas;
- curriculum development;
- updating/access to current thinking;
- impetus and enthusiasm;
- extra help;
- enjoyment.

Teachers described IT-INSET as having a number of advantages compared with hosting block teaching practice - sharing responsibility, learning from one another in a more relaxed atmosphere, acquiring new ideas, and giving the time and impetus to plan, observe, evaluate, discuss and rethink. On the other hand, they reported that block teaching practice provided more sustained contact with students, attention to a wider range of the curriculum, and more opportunity to spend time with individual children. They also found it less demanding.

Tutors' perceptions of benefit

Tutors were asked to 'Rate each of the forms of school experience on a scale from 1 (of no benefit whatsoever) to 6 (of maximum benefit) in terms of *how they helped you as a teacher to cater appropriately for children's learning.*' The mean ratings from sixty-seven tutors given in Table 10.5 indicate that tutors rated IT-INSET as the most beneficial form of school experience available to them.

Compared with supervising block teaching practice, tutors valued IT-INSET for the opportunities to work with children and to study their learning, to work collaboratively with teachers and students, to bring school and college concerns together, and to gain in acceptance and credibility. By contrast, tutors saw block teaching practice as providing them with closer contact with more individual students and with a broader range of experience of different schools.

From interviewing seventeen tutors from Training Institution 05, a seconded teacher reported tutors' perceived benefits of IT-INSET as:

- participation in the collaborative experience and discussions;
- the opportunity for relevant, up-to-date, practical experience;
- the opportunity for some tutors to teach a subject other than their own, which was considered to be good for the tutor's professional development and credibility;
- the provision of a good introduction to wider professional relationships;
- enjoyment of the challenge of the classroom;
- experience of the 'learning to learn' specialism as opposed to curriculum specialisms;
- acquisition and development of management skills.

Table 10.5   Tutors' views of various forms of school experience

Form of school experience	Mean rating
IT-INSET	5.02
Block secondment	4.33
Intermittent secondment	4.33
School-based INSET courses	4.24
School-based initial training courses	4.05
Consultancy/research	3.67
Teaching practice supervision	3.63

The following comments from tutors were typical:

The teachers and students taught me to listen more.
I was impressed by the excellent follow-up support by the teacher during the week.
Being accepted as a colleague was good for me.
There has been no other system that I have used in the college that has been so valuable.

Benefits to schools

Of the headteachers who responded to the questionnaire about IT-INSET in their schools, 93 per cent reported benefits of some kind interpreted in terms of the four levels of implementation of IT-INSET described in the previous chapter (pp. 119-120).

Level 3 - IT-INSET applied. 12 per cent of headteachers reported that teachers had developed their skills for the analysis and evaluation of pupil learning and that, beyond those teachers directly involved, the school and its curriculum had benefited from the IT-INSET focus on curriculum review. In other words, IT-INSET had acted as a stimulus to school development.

Level 2 - IT-INSET conceptualised. 19 per cent of headteachers reported that the teachers directly involved in the IT-INSET teams had developed their skills for reviewing the curriculum and analysing and evaluating pupils' learning. There had, however, been no extension to other staff of the school or into other areas of the curriculum.

Level 1 - IT-INSET done without understanding. 44 per cent of headteachers did not refer to skills for reviewing the curriculum in enumerating the gains for their schools in taking part in IT-INSET. Two-thirds of these thought that the teachers involved had derived a general INSET benefit in the shape of stimulation, refreshment or the acquisition of new ideas and 42 per cent thought that the curriculum in the class concerned had benefited. None of this suggests, however, that evaluation skills had been developed which would confer a continuing benefit.

Level 0 - Non-IT-INSET. 25 per cent of headteachers did not describe any benefit to the teachers, curriculum or school, either in the classes concerned or beyond. This is sufficient to suggest that real IT-INSET had not taken place since its central tenet is the combination of initial and in-service training.

Table 10.6 shows the responses of 180 headteachers to the question 'What is your assessment of the contribution of IT-INSET to your school?' grouped in terms of the four levels of outcome. It is noticeable from Table 10.6 that the number of benefits of all kinds reported by headteachers increased through the four levels of implementation: Level 3 headteachers reported five times as many benefits as Level 0 headteachers and over twice as many benefits as Level 1 headteachers.

Table 10.6 Benefits reported by headteachers

Benefit	Percentage of headteachers			
	Level 0 (45 heads)	Level 1 (80 heads)	Level 2 (34 heads)	Level 3 (21 heads)
Learning evaluation skills	0	0	100	100
Learning teamwork skills	0	8	15	38
Other professional benefits for teachers	0	69	53	71
Curriculum development	0	42	0	57
General stimulation	0	21	0	71
Enhanced pupil activity/learning	44	33	32	48
'Excellent, very worthwhile'	0	26	17	19
Positive input from students/tutors	9	11	17	14
Little effect on school	31	3	6	0
Benefited students	20	5	17	10
Students/tutors unhelpful	11	6	3	0
Generally negative	24	6	6	0
Average number of benefits reported	0.8	1.9	2.6	4.3

Benefits to training institutions

Sixteen principals or directors of training institutions responded to a questionnaire asking for their assessment of IT-INSET. Their small number precludes an analysis by levels of implementation, though inferences will be drawn in Chapter 11 which illuminate the role of training institutions in promoting various levels of implementation.

The principals'/directors' observations were very diverse although universally positive. Table 10.7 shows the frequency with which various benefits were mentioned.

Table 10.7   Benefits to training institutions

Benefit	No. of mentions
Created greater collaboration with their local education authorities	15
Promoted professional interchange	8
Enhanced appreciation of others' problems	5
Made a fundamental contribution to the development of initial training	5
Increased participants' contribution	4
Promoted examination of the theory/practice relationship in the course	3
Supported work in curriculum evaluation	3
Permeated other aspects of the course	3
Promoted observation and evaluation of pupils' learning	2
Changed tutors' teaching styles	2
Increased tutors' credibility	1
Improved attitudes to evaluation	1

Benefits to local education authorities

Eleven chief education officers replied to the IT-INSET questionnaire. Of these, five had little or no knowledge of the programme operating in their schools, usually because the training institution had worked unilaterally. The ways in which responding chief education officers perceived that IT-INSET had been beneficial are listed in Table 10.8.

The following extracts are taken from the replies of the two chief education officers who were most actively supportive of IT-INSET. They illustrate the potential benefits to local education authorities where there is such positive support.

Table 10.8   Benefits to local education authorities

Benefit	No. of mentions
Improving relationships with the local training institution	9
General ways	5
Promoting collaboration	5
Promoting curriculum development	4
Contributing to local education authorities' school-centred staff development policies	3
Strengthening whole-school approaches to curriculum evaluation and development	2
Increasing professional discussion	2
Facilitating INSET without disruption to classes	1
Breaking down individual teachers' isolation	1
Contributing to the local education authority's understanding and practice of school-focused and school-based INSET	1

In what ways, if at all, has IT-INSET benefited the schools involved (beyond any personal development for the teachers in whose classes IT-INSET began)?

It is in relation to 'impact' that the benefit for schools has to be evaluated. Within the Authority, various patterns of IT-INSET involvement have operated: in one school as many as five teams were operating simultaneously whereas in others it may have been only one or two. Certainly in the school which had five of its twenty-one classes involved simultaneously, much staffroom discussion and cross-fertilisation appeared to take place. Perhaps the most significant form of impact which has been observed to date is the increase in professional discussion and debate among the teachers.

Clearly the majority of these experiences have occurred within primary or special schools in which cross-fertilisation is often more common than in the more tightly structured secondary school. However, we have already some evidence of the interest of senior staff as a whole being aroused by the development of IT-INSET in a particular department of one secondary school.

With the development of school-focused INSET through our Grant-Related In-Service Training arrangements which place a considerable responsibility on the individual school for its own professional, curricular and institutional development, we would hope that IT-INSET would offer a highly cost-effective way forward. In this connection we are hoping to increase the level of dissemination of information concerning the scheme to a greater number of schools and teachers. *(CEO A)*

What effects has IT-INSET had on relationships between your authority and the training institution in INSET work generally?

The relationships between this Authority, the training institution and other local teacher training institutions are generally positive. Both at individual officer level and institutionally, the Authority and its teacher training partners have worked together successfully over a number of years. However, it is clear that the unique format of the IT-INSET programme offers a particular opportunity for such collaboration and this has been exemplified in, for example, the joint selection procedures which were adopted for the appointment of IT-INSET teacher-fellows in late 1986. That particular exercise also enabled a cross-collaboration between the Authority, voluntary colleges and the polytechnic and thus IT-INSET has not only strengthened individual ties but has helped support the growth of a corporate approach to professional development in advance of the centrally determined Grant-Related In-Service Training arrangements. *(CEO A)*

IT-INSET has, I would say, had the effect of reinforcing, consolidating and developing the relationships between our colleagues. There is a long tradition of excellent linkage between the [Training Institution] and the County Education Department, both at adviser and officer level. IT-INSET has built upon this tradition and has given coherence and direction to our mutually supportive school-focused approaches. It has contributed greatly to our understanding and practice of school-focused and school-based INSET. It has proved an excellent approach in identifying needs at a variety of levels -

teachers' needs, children's needs, school needs and local education authority needs. *(CEO B)*

What part has IT-INSET played in the overall INSET policy and programme in your authority?

IT-INSET and, indeed, the work of the Centre for Evaluation and Development in Teacher Education more generally have played a very important part in our overall strategy for INSET. I believe the aims of our respective approaches, as documented in Centre papers and in our INSET submission to the Department of Education and Science, are now consonant with each other. The practices of IT-INSET have had wide influence upon our approaches to school-focused INSET. This is not to suggest that there is not still a great deal to do. For example, we have yet to develop, in partnership with our schools, a really coherent policy for the induction of teachers new to the profession. The IT-INSET approach clearly would have potential for the professional development of teachers in their first years. We have yet to exploit this potential. *(CEO B)*

Summary

Team members, schools, training institutions and local education authorities appear to operate IT-INSET at one of four levels. With each successive level, there is an increase in the benefits to participants which IT-INSET is designed to confer. Figure 10.9 indicates the main characteristics of each level of implementation for each of the agencies involved.

At Level 0, the gains for local education authorities, training institutions and schools are negligible. Participants, including children, enjoy only the kind of experience with which all are familiar.

At Level 1, there is rudimentary co-operation between the training institution and the local education authority from which the latter gains little and the former derives some slightly enhanced INSET credibility for what is essentially an initial training exercise in the schools. The schools embark upon IT-INSET with some expectation of benefit, but are often disappointed because of the limited nature of the team's activity. Team members tend to gain to some extent from a modified form of teaching practice in which they enjoy more discussion and co-operation.

Level 2 is characterised by a shared understanding of the purposes of IT-INSET and thus all participants benefit from striving to collaborate in using observation and evaluation to develop the children's learning. New skills are learned and IT-INSET is seen to be a programme in its own right, distinctive from but complementary to teaching practice, as well as a valid INSET opportunity. The local education authority benefits from this injection into schools and the training institution gains a developing perception of the relevance of this range of professional skills to its teacher education courses generally.

At Level 3 that perception is acquired and generalised across local education authority, training institution, schools and team members, leading to a greater congruence or match between all parties about approaches to teacher education. The benefits of IT-INSET are exploited by everyone involved as tools in continuing professional and school development, rather than as ends in themselves, and the dynamic of multiplying benefit is established. Inevitably, pupils benefit in concert with adults and institutions since that is the rationale of the whole activity.

Table 10.9 Characteristics of the four levels of IT-INSET in LEAs, training institutions, schools and teams

Agency	Level 0 Non-IT-INSET	Level 1 Doing IT-INSET	Level 2 Conceptualising IT-INSET	Level 3 Applying IT-INSET
Local education authorities	Ignore IT-INSET.	Give approval to IT-INSET. Possibly discuss with training institution schools to be involved.	Understand teacher education function of IT-INSET. Negotiate and participate in planning and preparation.	Apply IT-INSET principles and process through INSET provision. Integrate IT-INSET into GRIST planning.
Training institutions	Use label 'IT-INSET' for school experience similar to teaching practice.	Organise IT-INSET placements, inform schools. Give minimal preparation to tutors, students and teachers.	Understand teacher education function of IT-INSET. Focus tutor, student and teacher preparation on purpose and skills of IT-INSET.	Apply IT-INSET principles and process through course. Make IT-INSET programmes integral to course. /cont.

Agency	Level 0 Non-IT-INSET	Level 1 Doing IT-INSET	Level 2 Conceptualising IT-INSET	Level 3 Applying IT-INSET
Schools	Host IT-INSET as favour to college. Perceive as student training.	Recognise general INSET potential of IT-INSET. Make organisational preparations.	Understand IT-INSET as INSET in collaborative curriculum review. Prepare teachers who will be involved.	Integrate IT-INSET into staff and curriculum development plans for the school.
Teams	Students practise teaching. Tutor and teacher advise.	Collaborate in planning, teaching and observing.	Collaborate in planning, teaching and evaluating, focus on pupil learning issue, share purpose and roles.	Understand and apply IT-INSET process in own professional development and curriculum development.

11

The influence of training institutions

The higher the level at which teams work in IT-INSET, the greater are the benefits to themselves, pupils, schools, training institutions, and local education authorities. This chapter is concerned with identifying those factors within the control of training institutions which appear to help and hinder progress towards higher level IT-INSET activity. It begins with an examination of a number of measures which indicate that the level of success achieved by teams tends to be determined by the training institution with which they are associated.

The remainder of the chapter considers the key differences between more and less successful training institutions in terms of four factors which helped and hindered effective IT-INSET practice by their teams:

- the match between the principles of IT-INSET and philosophy and practice in the initial training course;
- understanding of the philosophy and purposes of IT-INSET;
- the extent of planning within the training institution, particularly the preparation of participants;
- the effectiveness of collaboration with local education authorities.

The influence of training institutions on teams

Several measures revealed that the IT-INSET practice associated with each individual training institution tended to be preponderantly good, moderate or poor. (All training institutions which were involved in IT-INSET in 1986-87 were invited to complete all instruments, but problems with timing and the organisation of distribution and collection resulted in incomplete returns.) Four examples will be quoted here.

The four levels of observing and analysing classroom practice Table 11.1 shows the distribution of the four levels of observing and analysing classroom practice, derived from analysis of 247 individual team members' diary entries (pp. 119-20), between seven training institutions. The preponderance of Level 3 observation and analysis in Institutions 03, 25, 10 and 05 is striking, particularly by comparson with Institutions 09, 06 and 13.

Table 11.1   Percentage distribution of levels of observing and analysing practice across seven training institutions

Institution number	Level 0 %	Level 1 %	Level 2 %	Level 3 %
03	0	0	16	84
25	0	25	0	75
10	9	0	15	76
05	7	3	28	62
09	21	9	35	35
06	4	58	8	31
13	15	35	31	19

Teams' self-perceptions of their achievements Table 11.2 shows the relative positions of training institutions in relation to their teams' self-perceptions of their achievements, described in terms of the two factors[1] identified in Chapter 9 (p. 122). High achievement is associated with a negative value for the factor loading, and lower achievement with a positive value. The twelve institutions are ranked in terms of their scores on each factor separately.

It can be seen that three training institutions - 03, 07 and 25 - fall in the top half of the rankings (1-6) on both Factor 1, the general achievement factor, and Factor 2, the basic processes factor. Another three instututions - 08, 10 and 15 - fall in the lower half of the rankings (7-12) on both factors.

Table 11.2   Relative positions of twelve training institutions for their loadings on self-perception of achievements

Institution number	Loading Factor 1	Rank Factor 1	Loading Factor 2	Rank Factor 2
09	-1.08	1	0.36	10
11	-0.70	2	-0.04	7
07	-0.22	3	-0.41	2
25	-0.22	4	-0.19	5
03	-0.16	5	-0.22	4
13	-0.14	6	0.34	9
08	0.01	7	1.50	12
06	0.06	8	-0.17	6
10	0.19	9	0.21	8
18	0.43	10	-0.14	3
02	0.76	11	-0.63	1
15	0.96	12	0.80	11

Number of disqualifiers Table 11.3 shows the average number of disqualifiers (p. 127) per training institution arising from team questionnaire items indicating practice inconsistent with IT-INSET. The relatively high number of disqualifiers for institutions 14, 08, 15 and 02 is noticeable, as also is the relatively low number of disqualifiers for institutions 03 and 25, both of which scored highly on the two preceding measures.

The contribution of IT-INSET to schools Table 11.4 is based on 180 responses to the item in the headteachers' questionnaire which asked, 'What is your assessment of the contribution of IT-INSET to your school?' Responses from headteachers associated with each institution were categorised by means of the four levels of IT-INSET practice described in Chapter 9 (pp. 119-20). Once again, there are striking differences between institutions.

Training institution rankings Inspection of Tables 11.1-11.4 suggests that, on the whole, individual institutions tended to be in broadly the same category across different measures. The national evaluation provided data which enabled comparisons between training institutions to be made on a total of eight different measures, although not all measures are available for all training institutions. Table 11.5 shows the rank order of institutions based on their mean ranking on at least six of these eight measures.

Table 11.3   Average number of disqualifiers for thirteen institutions

Institution number	Average number of disqualifiers*
12	0.0
09	1.3
25	1.8
03	1.9
06	2.0
11	2.1
18	2.4
13	2.6
10	3.7
14	5.5
08	5.8
15	6.7
02	7.0

* The higher frequency of disqualifiers in institutions 02, 08 and 15 is significant at the $p<0.001$ level.

Match of IT-INSET with the initial training course

A training institution is likely to be more successful in implementing IT-INSET if its existing philosophy and practice of teacher education match well with the principles of IT-INSET. The significant elements are emphasis on a problem-solving approach to developing teaching skills, open discussion of issues in teaching and learning, and collaborative relationships between tutors, students and teachers. Where these exist, tutors and students are more likely to have appropriate expectations of IT-INSET and to have more of the requisite cognitive and social skills. Thus institutions successful in IT-INSET tend to have some or all of the following:

Table 11.4 Percentage of headteachers associated with eighteen training institutions reporting contributions of IT-INSET to their schools at different levels

Institution number	Level 0 %	Level 1 %	Level 2 %	Level 3 %
10	22	22	34	22
06	6	44	25	25
11	25	33	17	25
25	43	14	43	0
01	0	66	34	0
08	43	29	29	0
03	11	63	21	5
13	33	42	17	8
02	39	39	13	9
05	40	40	10	10
07	50	30	10	10
15	20	60	0	20
04	18	37	18	0
09	17	66	17	0
14	0	100	0	0
12	50	50	0	0
16	50	50	0	0
18	100	0	0	0

• re-designed initial training courses with an underpinning philosophy of practical theorising, giving rise to the practice of independent study, classroom enquiry and evaluation;
• teacher-tutor, teacher partnership, or supervisory teacher schemes which give teachers responsibility *vis-à-vis* students and in which teachers are regarded as having expertise which is complementary to that of tutors and equally valuable;
• flexible INSET arrangements of various kinds, including school-based collaboration, in which shared enquiry into the quality of pupil learning figures prominently;
• arrangements for constructive contact of tutors with schools and teachers as a continuing and essential part of tutors' own professional development.

Table11.5   Rank order of training institutions

Institution number	Mean rank
25	3.2
03	3.7
11	4.1
07	4.5
06	5.3
09	5.9
08	7.4
10	7.4
13	7.6
02	8.4
18	8.6
15	11.0

By contrast, it appears likely that, where the level of IT-INSET operation is consistently low across an institution, IT-INSET is at variance with the philosophy and practice of the initial training course. Tutors and students then apparently either fail to understand the purposes of IT-INSET or lack the skills to work in a way that can yield the intended benefits.

Understanding of the philosophy and purposes of IT-INSET

The paramount factor in determining the level at which teams work is the quality of understanding of the philosophy and purposes of IT-INSET on the part of those responsible for the overall organisation of the programme. For example, the following characteristics are marked in successful training institutions.

• Recognition of IT-INSET, not simply as an alternative form of school experience, but as a teacher education process which has implications for all of the training institution's initial and in-service programmes. This may imply, for example, that school-based work in the initial training course is being extended, that new modular awards are being developed for teachers, that the nature of the presentation of educational theory in the initial training course is being fundamentally reconsidered, that the initial training course is being more extensively linked to INSET, and that collaboration with the local education authority is being developed in various ways. Most importantly, all of such activities are designed to develop the twin processes of collaboration and practical theorising.

- Recognition of the continuing need to explore and enhance understanding of the IT-INSET teacher education process. Successful IT-INSET institutions have been conspicuously active in, for example, maintaining contact with the Centre for Evaluation and Development in Teacher Education, using Centre staff for their own development and evaluation activities, using Centre literature, attending and hosting national meetings concerned with IT-INSET issues, seconding local people to study at the Centre and making individual contacts for discussion purposes with other IT-INSET institutions.

The major factor inhibiting progress in IT-INSET is a misunderstanding in the training institution of IT-INSET's philosophy and purposes. In some institutions this amounts to a fundamental misinterpretation of the programme and team members are advised to engage in activities which actually preclude achieving the intrinsic benefits of IT-INSET. The following are examples.

- The teacher chooses a curriculum topic for co-operative teaching rather than an issue in children's learning for collaborative evaluation.
- Following limited joint discussion, the students do the bulk of the planning and the work with the children.
- Observation is non-existent or cursory.
- The teacher and tutor subsequently advise and/or assess the students on their teaching performances.
- The team comment impressionistically, if at all, on the pupils' response to a lesson and then pool ideas drawn from previous experience to plan the next lesson.

In these circumstances, students are exposed to a poor model of taking teaching decisions and the teacher and tutor gain little or no INSET benefit. Effectively, teams are not doing IT-INSET but something more akin to an alternative form of teaching practice. In the words of one seconded teacher, reporting observation of IT-INSET in twelve schools associated with Training Institution 02 (which ranked low in Table 11.5) and interviews with twelve headteachers, twenty-seven teachers and twelve tutors:

> Benefits to the teachers were seen, by most tutors, as being incidental spin-offs of the process. Tutors' primary concern, it was felt, was the experience of the students. When team members were asked how they saw the teachers' role in the project, many responded in an way that expressed support of a comment by a tutor that 'The teacher's principal role is as a resource to help plan and provide.'

In a small minority of institutions, there is limited understanding of IT-INSET but teams are clearly advised to undertake appropriate activities, i.e. collaborative planning, teaching and observing. In these instances, all team members play an equal part in the classroom work and ensuing discussion, they do make observations and they attempt to work democratically. However, there seems to be an inadequate appreciation of the purpose of working in this way and observations are often unused, evaluations not attempted and the team becomes an unreflective teaching unit.

Planning and preparation of participants

The provision of adequate and appropriate preparation of tutors, students, schools and teachers is absolutely critical. One seconded teacher, who observed IT-INSET in sixteen schools associated with Training Institution 05, and interviewed seventeen headteachers and fifteen teachers, noted:

> There is no doubt that the dissemination of information about IT-INSET to participants - theory, practice and organisation - allied to careful team selection and subsequent preparation can make or break an IT-INSET programme.

Effective preparation includes:

* communicating the purposes of IT-INSET clearly to tutors and students and advising them to undertake those activities which will yield the greatest benefits (i.e. concentrating on an issue

concerning pupils' learning, organising observation of pupils' learning, arranging time for systematic evaluation after each classroom session, planning future work in the light of this evaluation, and doing all of this as a collaborative process drawing on the expertise and ideas of all team members);

- communicating the purposes and practice of IT-INSET clearly to headteachers and teachers and, if necessary in conjunction with the local education authority, assisting headteachers in making appropriate preparations in their schools;
- providing adequate time and opportunities for all team members to clarify their understanding of IT-INSET and to establish their mutual expectations of the programme;
- providing adequate time and opportunity for individual teams to establish their joint purposes and to begin planning before work starts in the classroom.

The more successful training institutions have employed some or all of the following means to assist the preparation of participants:

- offering supplementary courses for students, tutors and teachers dealing with, for example, observation skills, practical evaluation, and discussion skills;
- organising pre-IT-INSET meetings for future participants, introducing the purposes of IT-INSET and giving time for team exploration and preliminary planning;
- using videos and documentation to provide introductory briefing on IT-INSET, as well as for subsequent reference.

In the words of a seconded teacher who conducted interviews with fourteen teachers working with Training Institution 03:

> Teachers who went into [the training institution] in the Autumn Term to discuss the investigation were able to launch into the project in the first designated week. Consultations and planning involving the whole team, supported by documentation on the principles of IT-INSET, led to committed and confident participation. Documentation was discussed several times during the experience - a practice which seemed to consolidate and focus understanding.

Where a training institution's understanding of the purposes of IT-INSET is limited, or practical problems have not been resolved, the preparation of team members and of schools tends to be misguided or inadequate and their progress is consequently inhibited. For example, almost a quarter of headteachers had no expectation that IT-INSET would benefit the school or its teachers in any way: in such circumstances, they are very much less likely to make preparations in the school that will facilitate the purposes of IT-INSET.

Many of the evaluation reports by seconded teachers emphasise the need for more extensive preparation of participants. For example:

In looking back on an IT-INSET experience a lot of team members felt better preparation would have been helpful - preparation in the form of understanding the principles and aims of IT-INSET and how to build working relationships. This applied to team members who had either a good or not so good experience. *(Interviews and observation of teams, Training Institutions 01 and 25)*

There was a legacy of misconceptions and unrealistic expectations evidenced by some of the headteachers about to take part in IT-INSET. For whatever reasons schools are selected or however careful the selection, the most crucial factor in initiating IT-INSET with a reasonable expectation of success is that its purpose and philosophy is clearly understood and transmitted to all levels of the educational structure so that they can respond in kind. *(Interviews with fourteen headteachers and forty-five class teachers, Training Institution 04)*

Team issue/focus/topic: This is being misinterpreted as the basis for classroom activity rather than the focus for curriculum evaluation and development. This can lead to an erosion of the basic strategy for IT-INSET ... I learned that the opportunity to observe can also suffer from this erosion of basic strategy. IT-INSET is about sharing teaching and observation in the classroom. Neglecting the observation component seriously reduces the INSET benefits to the teacher. In the majority of cases teachers were not clear that the project set out to develop their observational skills (although many capitalised on the opportunity to do so). I found no evidence of systematic observation and recording. Without systematic observation supporting a defined focus, any progression towards curriculum evaluation and development often becomes based on conjecture and prejudice. I did not see, at any time, a structured discussion. By 'structured' I mean where a chairperson was elected, an agenda used, reports given, and records made. No team had identified at the outset a common curriculum focus for evaluation and development. It is possible that a clear focus for observation could demonstrate the need for a more systematic approach to the discussion. *(Observation of IT-INSET in twelve schools and interviews with twelve headteachers, twenty-seven class teachers and twelve tutors, Training Institution 02)*

Collaboration with local education authorities

It may seem odd that the extent and nature of collaboration between training institutions and local education authorities is described as a helping or hindering factor within the control of training institutions. Collaboration is, of course, a two-way process, but experience of IT-INSET has often been that it is a training institution, rather than a local education authority, which takes the initiative in implementing IT-INSET. The burden of ensuring effective collaboration therefore commonly falls on the training institution.

Close collaboration between a training institution and its local education authority (or authorities) includes:

- joint clarification of the purposes of IT-INSET;
- mutual recognition of the function of collaborative curriculum review in school development and of its equal importance for students, teachers and tutors;
- recognition that IT-INSET benefits local education authorities and training institutions reciprocally and that either can impede or enhance the benefits for the other;
- joint overall planning and evaluation of IT-INSET programmes so that the potential benefits are maximised for local education authority and training institution participants;
- joint communication with schools so that teachers recognise the value placed upon the IT-INSET processes of collaborative curriculum review by the local education authority;
- provision of supply cover for teachers engaged in IT-INSET so that they can take a full part in team evaluations and thus enhance their skills for collaborative curriculum review.

The three most successful IT-INSET institutions (25, 03 and 11 in Table 11.5) have particularly strong links with their local education authorities. These links take some or all of the forms of:

- continuing discussions of INSET policy and plans by the local education authority and the training institution and exploration of reciprocal support;
- discussions about prospective changes in the initial training course and the opportunities for combining those with various forms of INSET;
- regular meetings between the institution and the local education authority to develop and monitor IT-INSET and contingent developments such as further, related INSET activities for teachers;
- annual preparation by the institution of a bid to the local education authority for supply cover for teachers involved in IT-INSET;
- release by the local education authority of teachers to evaluate IT-INSET under the joint guidance of the training institution and the authority;
- release by the local education authority of teachers to tutor IT-INSET teams to supplement the training institution's permanent staff;
- promotion by the local education authority of the philosophy and practice of IT-INSET at a range of INSET meetings;
- initiation of meetings by the local education authority for headteachers and teachers involved in IT-INSET to evaluate progress and discuss further developments;
- attendance by local education authority advisers and officers at national IT-INSET meetings in company with their training institution counterparts;
- joint interviewing by the local education authority and the training institution of applicants for appropriate award-bearing courses;
- the evolution of a shared teacher education philosophy with agreed practical consequences so that, for example, the local education authority earmarks secondments for INSET courses tailored to meet specific professional needs.

Where such collaboration exists, it is evident that headteachers and teachers are much more likely to have appropriate expectations of IT-INSET, to prepare accordingly, and thus to facilitate the operation of IT-INSET at the highest level.

Maximum development of IT-INSET is manifestly inhibited by lack of collaboration between the training institution and its local education authority. At worst, local education authorities have not known that IT-INSET was in progress in their schools. At an only marginally better level, local education authorities have merely been asked permission for IT-INSET to be offered to schools.

Some local education authorities have been resistant to training institutions' best efforts to collaborate with them. It may be that they have dismissed IT-INSET as essentially an initial training exercise or have regarded any INSET element as merely peripheral. Either suggests a lack of understanding of the purposes of IT-INSET and perhaps also a lack of emphasis on school-based collaborative curriculum review. One seconded teacher, referring to Training Institution 05's relationship with its local education authority, wrote:

> The extent of involvement of advisers during the period that IT-INSET was functioning in schools seems generally to have been slight, with little or no contact between the advisory service and teams in schools. This was a pity since schools and their staffs, and the college participants too, would appreciate some visible sign of local education authority support for the project.

Another, referring to Training Institution 04, commented:

> Collaborative evaluation needs participation by the whole team. Participation by the whole team necessitates the provision of supply cover to release members from teaching commitments. The local education authority does not provide supply cover.

Where collaboration between training institutions and local education authorities does not exist, there are several detrimental consequences for the level at which IT-INSET operates.

- Headteachers and teachers are more likely to interpret IT-INSET as substantially initial training with little or no INSET potential, thus adversely affecting the quality of teachers' contributions to teams.
- The training institution is prevented from developing a wider perception of the role of IT-INSET in school development and is

obliged to operate the programme in a way which makes a limited INSET contribution, thus restricting the learning opportunities of all team members.

- Teachers are not provided with supply cover to enable them to take part in team evaluations, with consequent limitations on their own professional development and that of the other team members.

Note

1. The two factors together account for 58% of the total variance.

12

Further helping and hindering factors

As indicated in the previous chapter, the training institution is the single greatest influence on the quality of IT-INSET practice. But there are other influences also, and this final chapter summarising the findings of the national evaluation examines those helping and hindering factors that result from the influences of tutors, headteachers and the teams themselves.

The tutors

Tutors tend to be the most influential members of teams. Analysis of diary entries shows that both teacher and student members of teams tend to work at the same level as their tutor (Tables 12.1 and 12.2). By contrast, if the teacher works at a higher level, this appears not to influence the students.

A major factor in a tutor's effectiveness is his or her understanding of the philosophy and purpose of IT-INSET and willingness to work appropriately with the team. This includes:

- focusing on the learning of the particular class of pupils and collaborating in gathering specific evidence of learning, in making evaluations and in planning specific developments, rather than providing general, externally-derived solutions untested in the particular context;
- demonstrating regard for evidence, rational thinking, logical argument, the use of theorising and theory, and valuing the contribution of all other team members;
- developing a tutoring style which sets standards for the conduct of the programme but devolves responsibility to the team

collectively so that everyone has the opportunity to learn the necessary cognitive and social skills.

Table 12.1   Percentages of students, grouped by tutor level, achieving Levels 0-3 in respect of observing and analysing practice

Tutor level	Number of tutors	Percentage of students working at levels:				Number of students
		0	1	2	3	
3	16	13	4	9	74	47
2	7	5	5	60	30	20
1	2	0	50	25	25	8
0	2	14	0	57	29	7

Table 12.2   Percentages of teachers, grouped by tutor level, achieving Levels 0-3 in respect of observing and analysing practice

Tutor level	Number of tutors	Percentage of teachers working at levels:				Number of teachers
		0	1	2	3	
3	16	4	48	13	75	24
2	7	10	0	50	40	10
1	2	0	100	0	0	1
0	0	0	0	0	0	0

These desirable tutor characteristics are extrapolated from the logic of IT-INSET and the evidence of the national evaluation. Since the characteristics are those which IT-INSET is centrally concerned to develop and since tutor example is demonstrably important in forming teams' expectations of themselves and the process in which they are engaged, it follows that effective IT-INSET tutors are manifestly in possession of these characteristics.

By the same argument, it is assumed that unsuccessful tutors are likely to have a less than adequate understanding of the philosophy and purposes of IT-INSET. This problem is exacerbated in some institutions which have had to require unwilling tutors to take part in IT-INSET.

A second factor in a tutor's effectiveness is his or her level of commitment to an appropriate tutor role. Headteachers, teachers and students made clear to seconded teachers that the tutor's contribution to the team is particularly significant. The tutor is responsible for helping team colleagues to understand the practical implications of the IT-INSET philosophy, for establishing collaborative relationships, and for developing an energetic sense of purpose and direction. This is not regarded as detrimental to team democracy but rather as the tutor's particular share in the joint responsibility.

The following quotations from seconded teachers' evaluation reports on successful tutors illustrate this.

> Some class teachers openly stated that the role of the tutor was vital - their open enthusiasm acting as a driving force, or quieter interest attracting a keen response. Typical comments from teachers were:
>   Positive, supportive and quietly dynamic.
>   Instrumental in getting things done.
>   Concerned.
>   Vivacious, a magnetic personality.
>   Sympathetic and loved teaching.
> *(Training Institutions 01 and 25)*

> Of the ten schools, six commented that the quality of the tutor was highly contributory to the success of the team. Criteria mentioned were:
> • An awareness of the philosophy of primary education;
> • Past experience in primary schools;
> • Understanding of IT-INSET;
> • Where the teams came closest to the IT-INSET model, the tutors demonstrated that it is possible to strike a balance between that of 'partner in learning' and 'student educator'. *(Training Institution 02)*

Comment must be made on the dedication of IT-INSET tutors in endeavouring against many odds to achieve good IT-INSET practice. *(Training Institution 10)*

There is no doubt that the most successful tutors quickly established close working relationships with the school, while the least successful left the teacher to fill too many gaps. The majority of schools were extremely appreciative of and impressed by the tutor. Some teachers expected the tutor to sit back, watch and then come up with words of wisdom. They were surprised therefore when tutors rolled up their sleeves and got on with the job! Three teachers spoke of the impressive performance of enthusiastic tutors tackling problems, not in their specialist areas, with professional dedication. In one particular case the support of the tutor did not end on the last day of IT-INSET but continued in various tangible forms and this was greatly appreciated by the school. There can be no doubt that team members enjoyed the greatest benefits from IT-INSET where the 'tutor' image - and, to a lesser extent, the 'teacher' image - were successfully broken down. *(Training Institution 05)*

By contrast, the following are some typical examples of seconded teachers' observations on less successful tutors.

The resentment caused among school staff by the intermittent appearance of some tutors has already been noted. In IT-INSET, participants operate as a collaborative team, the success of which depends on the level of commitment of each of its members. Experience has shown that where the level of commitment of such a crucial member as the tutor is high then the likelihood of a successful outcome is enhanced. Conversely where commitment is low then the whole venture is put under strain and the enterprise is likely to founder. Among tutors actually taking part, levels of involvement varied greatly. Reasons for this are not known but it has been suggested that other training institution commitments, lack of perceived benefits to themselves, and misunderstandings about role were among the possible causes. *(Training Institution 04)*

The tutor's role as co-ordinator for the college-based members of the team is an important one throughout the whole of the

IT-INSET period but the tutor has a particularly crucial part to play in the early stages. He or she must liaise, inform, initiate, suggest, stimulate, organise and reassure. For some tutors all this came as second nature, for others it was not so easy. *(Training Institution 05)*

In some teams there was less equality of status. An individual (normally the tutor) would dominate the early discussion sessions, leading the discussion and in so doing electing themselves chairperson. If this situation was not corrected by an early agreement to rotate this role, a lack of equality - or reduced equality - existed. In the case of one team there was a collective student opinion that the tutor's initial 'I know best' attitude marred team relations throughout the experience. *(Training Institution 03)*

Non-training institution tutors The evidence of the national evaluation suggests that effective IT-INSET tutors need not necessarily be members of staff of a training institution. In some cases, a programme cannot be adequately staffed from within the institution. Additional tutors have been recruited from among teachers seconded to the training institution for further study and specially prepared for an IT-INSET tutoring role, from teachers experienced in IT-INSET who have been released by their local education authorities from their schools to act as tutors, from teachers or headteachers working with teams in their own schools, and from among advisers and advisory teachers. The performance of all of these as IT-INSET tutors has compared well with that of training institution staff.

Headteachers

Schools are initially dependent for the level at which their IT-INSET programmes operate on the training institution and its understanding of IT-INSET, its collaboration with the local education authority, its preparation of team members, its communication with headteachers, and the quality of its tutors.

It can be seen from Table 12.3, based on 180 completed questionnaires from headteachers, that they tend to make fuller and more appropriate preparations for IT-INSET if they have a clear expectation of its specific benefits. Table 12.4 shows that there is also a relationship between the quality and kind of preparations made by headteachers and the level reached by the IT-INSET programme in their schools.

Table 12.3   Percentage of headteachers making different preparations for a forthcoming IT-INSET programme grouped by expectations

Preparations	No expectations of INSET (% of 54 heads)	Expectations of general INSET (% of 101 heads)	Expectations appropriate to IT-INSET (% of 25 heads)
Attended meetings at training institution	15	22	40
Held team meetings in school	25	22	28
Tutor visited school	37	24	40
Students visited school	19	11	24
Organised space/ time	13	27	24
Planned work for pupils	10	16	20
Discussed with participating teachers	23	28	36
Helped to identify issue for IT-INSET	21	22	24
Discussed with whole staff	12	27	40
Discussed IT-INSET process	8	21	28

Team members were asked to note in their evaluation diaries the factors which they thought had helped and hindered the progress of their team. They listed a very great diversity of factors, but only four were mentioned in 20 per cent or more of the 247 diaries. Two of these appear to be related directly or indirectly to the headteacher and his or her preparations for and support of the programme:

- 22 per cent of team members referred to a positive and welcoming school climate as having helped their team progress;
- 20 per cent referred to the positive attitude and energetic involvement of the class teacher.

Table 12.4   Percentages of headteachers at each programme level   who had made different preparations

Preparations	Level 0 (% of 45 heads)	Level 1 (% of 80 heads)	Level 2 (% of 34 heads)	Level 3 (% of 21 heads)
Attended meetings at training institution	22	23	24	43
Held team meetings in school	16	21	29	38
Tutor visited school	38	29	26	19
Students visited school	22	11	15	10
Organised space/ time	11	21	29	38
Planned work for pupils	11	20	12	5
Discussed with parti- cipating teachers	20	28	38	24
Helped to identify issue for IT-INSET	20	19	32	12
Discussed with whole staff	16	23	24	48
Discussed IT-INSET process	7	19	32	38

The following successful headteacher activities were identified by the evaluation.

1. *Preparing teachers for school-based INSET* This included:

- discussing the purpose of IT-INSET with the teacher(s) who would be involved and helping them to clarify their expectations of the programme and their role within it;
- emphasising the INSET dimension of the programme;
- discussing the purpose of IT-INSET with the whole staff and identifying ways in which the benefits of the programme could extend beyond the teacher(s) directly involved.

2. *Helping in the identification of the team's issue* This entailed assisting in identifying, but not determining, the issue in pupils' learning which will be the focus of the team's work. (If the teacher is to gain maximum benefit then he or she must be convinced of the importance of the issue).

3. *Facilitating the programme* This involved:

- facilitating any necessary re-arrangements of time, space and classes to enable the team to work effectively;
- securing supply cover if it is available and ensuring that it is used to benefit the team;
- if supply cover is not available, making the fullest internal arrangements possible to release teacher(s) to take part in team evaluation sessions each week;
- creating a welcoming climate in the school for the external team members, assisting them in recognising their potential contribution to the development of the school and facilitating contact between them and other members of the staff.

4. *Anticipating staff and curriculum development* This involved:

- maintaining contact with the programme in progress so that the extension of its benefits through the school can be facilitated;
- recognising and valuing the enhanced skills of the teacher(s) involved and seeking to make use of them.

5. *Evaluating the programme* This entailed informing the tutor and/or training institution of the school's evaluation of the programme and recommendations for its future development if it is to benefit the school further.

The following unsuccessful headteacher activities were identified by the evaluation.

1. *Failing to help teachers to recognise IT-INSET as school-based INSET* If the teacher-members of teams did not recognise the programme as an INSET opportunity and perceived it as a form of initial training in which they took up their accustomed role, the lack of appropriate teacher involvement hampered the rest of the team.

2. *Unilaterally deciding upon the team's focus* If headteachers determined the focus for the team's work and did not take into account the wishes or interests of the teacher-members of teams, teachers inevitably tended not to be personally involved in the subsequent activities.

3. *Regarding the team as a disruption* Some headteachers regarded the external members of the team as a burden undertaken for the sake of the training institution, creating an unwelcoming climate which undermined the confidence and commitment of the team. If teams were isolated from the rest of the staff and were required to take their breaks away from the staffroom, both teams and staff regarded the programme as having nothing to do with the school beyond the individual classrooms involved and thus no extension of value to the school was possible.

4. *Taking no interest in the team's work* Some headteachers were consistently unavailable for consultation and such apparent lack of interest in teams' activities had a depressing effect upon the morale of all team members including the teachers.

5. *Not facilitating the team's work* Headteachers sometimes made less than maximum effort to arrange cover for teachers involved so that they were unable to attend team meetings, or the team was always incomplete while members covered classes in turn.

Teams

As shown in Chapter 9, teams vary from effectively not doing IT-INSET in any recognisable form to carrying through a programme from which they reap a measure of benefit in respect of most of the six skill areas. Though members of any one team are not identical in achievement, there tends to be a characteristic level of performance across the team.

Their level of achievement is strongly influenced by their training institution, the measure of involvement of their local education authority, their tutor and their headteacher and school. Nevertheless, teams still determine a large measure of their own success or lack of it.

The national evaluation provided evidence that the key characteristics of successful teams are:

- discussion of the philosophy and purposes of IT-INSET;
- focus upon a clear issue in the pupils' learning;
- joint clarification of the team's focus;
- exchanging the classroom roles to be taken each week by team members;
- taking joint responsibility for planning classroom work;
- planning jointly what and how to observe;
- sharing the teaching;
- making structured observations;
- having an explicit agenda for evaluation meetings;
- rotating the roles of discussion leader and minute taker among all members;
- having the minimum of an hour for team discussion each week;
- analysing pupils' learning;
- raising issues and questions concerning both the pupils' observed learning and the IT-INSET processes of collaborative evaluation and development;
- maintaining the focus on evaluating pupils' learning throughout the programme;
- sharing a common purpose and being equally committed;
- all contributing ideas and willing to learn from one another;
- being democratic.

These characteristics of successful teams are elaborated by the following observations by seconded teachers.

At times when the team was most in accord with the model, I witnessed (in discussions):
- openness of team members - each member being confident in exposing his or her beliefs, emotions and intellect to the scrutiny of both colleagues and strangers;

- the ability to articulate perceived children's needs and to justify pupils' tasks;
- an acceptance of the notion that all team members' views are of value, and that the range of experiences, skills and knowledge can be incorporated into a sharing of energy, enthusiasm and ideas;
- a willingness of all team members to listen;
- a rejection of the view that one or more members are exemplars of good practice and knowledge which has to be imparted to others.

(Training Institution 02)

Participants' views of helping factors were as follows:
- A shared philosophy and open-mindedness
- The quality and commitment of participants
- Positive attitudes
- Good personal relationships
- A supportive school - not just the head and class teacher
- A school with clearly defined needs
- A feeling of equality among team members
- A feeling of sharing the same experience for mutual benefit
- Teams of optimum size.

(Training Institution 05)

Team factors:
- A teacher who was supportive and sensitive to all team members and who was prepared to trust the soundness of the collective decision process in relation to the pupils
- The alternation of classroom responsibilities (teaching and observing) and clearly defined, rotating discussion and planning responsibilities (chairing or minuting meetings)
- An approach on the part of a tutor that was non-threatening in its openness, covert/overt guidance and humour
- A group of students who had already successfully worked together as a team on another aspect of their studies
- The team that reported the most successful experience were favoured with an appropriate balance and schedule of teaching and discussion time
- Teams made up of smaller numbers appeared to have freer, more open discussions with more equality in contributions.

(Training Institution 03)

In summary, the critical factors in making progress in IT-INSET are good understanding of its philosophy and purposes among all involved, effective communication among all participants, efficient practical planning, genuine collaboration, and willingness on the part of all participants to learn higher order professional skills with the intention of enhancing pupils' learning currently and in the future.

The key characteristics of less successful teams are:

- an erroneous or only partial understanding of the purposes of IT-INSET;
- lack of commitment to working as a team, agreeing specific purposes and sharing roles and responsibilities;
- allowing one or more members to dominate discussion;
- allowing members overtly or covertly to take unilateral action;
- not focusing on the pupils' learning and using the opportunity either to experiment with teaching methods without regard to the pupils' proven advantage or to engage in classroom research for their own purposes (for example, to provide the material for student dissertations);
- teacher and tutor adopting traditional roles as teacher trainers and students as trainees so that none are learning professional skills for collaborative curriculum review;
- failing to plan observations and other means of data collection so that there is only haphazard evidence on which to base evaluations;
- losing sight of the team's focus and purposes and not regularly re-establishing them;
- not organising discussions to make the best use of limited time;
- not airing team difficulties.

Some of these characteristics of less successful teams are elaborated in the following reports by seconded teachers.

Hindering factors:
- Poor personal relations within the group
- Poor teamwork - unequal status within the group - difficulty for some students to feel that they were equal partners in the team - this was felt more where the tutor was also the students' specialist tutor in a curriculum area

- Misunderstanding of the purpose and philosophy of IT-INSET by teachers who consider it to be another teaching practice (but so did some students)
- Absenteeism
- Dominant, negative or unreliable team members
- The attitude of some students who do not realise or cannot accept that IT-INSET is a 'special' situation - something different in initial training and INSET provision - this leads to their rating IT-INSET very low in their priorities and a less beneficial programme to all participants.

Observation seems to be a key issue with any IT-INSET programme. Two-thirds of all participants said that they felt it was very important, and a number of groups admitted that observation was one of the most difficult areas, mainly because of the width of interpretation. Most students mentioned the value of observing others at work in a teaching situation, yet the frequency with which observation was deliberately raised in discussion varied enormously. Some groups totally ignored observation. Some did not have an observer during IT-INSET sessions, for example, while others tended not to appreciate the value of developing their observation skills in order to increase their understanding of classroom practice. *(Training Institution 05)*

A great deal of printed matter flowed from the College to IT-INSET participants, but what did participants do with it? Headteachers and teachers all said that they had seen the information. Few, however, seemed clear about the contents and it was suspected, particularly in the light of what had happened, that generally it had not been studied in depth, if at all. The students said that they had not found the literature useful and probably would not read it. The booklets produced by the Centre for Evaluation and Development in Teacher Education, in particular, seemed to be 'trying to get a bit more complicated than we want.' What was needed, they thought, was a booklet that was 'simple and clearly presented with reasonable size print and pictures.' *(Training Institution 04)*

If some members were not committed to the work, the chances of a successful working team were threatened. A lack of enthusiasm or lack of realisation of the type and amount of work involved made it difficult for a team to function successfully as a united force:

- Everyone needs to realise that all members have a contribution to make - often there was too much hesitancy or no participation;
- Teams have to be committed to their work and attitude is all-important.

Some teams found it difficult to establish equality. This was felt to be due to a lack of understanding of the principles of IT-INSET, lack of commitment to work together, or simply not enough time. Where groups [of children] were formed from the start and kept throughout, it could lead to rigidity and isolation of work and planning. Group 'teachers' tended to be concerned only with the one small group and hardly to be aware of other groups. However, in some teams, even while working on a common theme, group teachers planned independently, interpreting their work in their own particular way. This could lead to a stilted discussion of work as others did not always find it easy to discuss work which they had no part in planning or observing. Add to this the fact that some teachers remained with the same group of children throughout, and the interest in other peoples' problems and difficulties sometimes seemed minimal. *(Training Institutions 01 and 25)*

A collaborative approach to curriculum evaluation and development, in an atmosphere of teamwork, is greatly affected by interpersonal social skills. Rigidity, suspicion, indifference and misunderstanding hinder the process and steps should be taken to minimise these. *(Training Institution 02)*

In summary, the most disabling factor in undertaking IT-INSET is a lack of understanding of its purposes and, in particular, of the role of collaborative curriculum review in teacher and school development and of the cognitive skills and interpersonal relationships which it requires. Beyond that, progress in IT-INSET is most inhibited by a lack of practical planning and preparation by teams so that team members can learn the requisite skills and exploit their opportunities to the full.

Conclusion

13

The present and future of IT-INSET

IT-INSET is a form of teacher education, both initial and in-service, which takes its nature and direction from the concept of teaching as implemented theorising. All teaching acts, even the apparently most intuitive, reflect teachers' theories about the relationship between means and ends. Theories vary in degree of articulation, comprehensiveness, basis in evidence, and even in consciousness. Theorising is dynamic and even the most habitual, taken-for-granted, bases for action are subject to modification. Practical theorising makes use of a range of sources: while experience is probably the most compelling, the initial training course, INSET programmes, colleagues, parents, further study and the media all provide material from which teachers create their personal understanding and interpretation of what they do.

Given this view of teaching, teacher education must concern itself centrally with theorising and with the processes by which experience and 'external theory' are conceptualised, analysed and synthesised into personal foundations for action open to continuing, rational modification. Traditionally, teacher education has probably been much more concerned with providing the raw material of experience, external theory, notions of good practice and curriculum solutions than with improving the cognitive processes by which each student and each teacher develops the personal understanding which better informs action.

Practice and improvement of theorising are equally appropriate for students, teachers and tutors. There is not a point for anyone when theorising has been completed and can ossify. Improving theorising requires different perspectives, fresh thoughts and different interpretations of events: combining those of experienced teachers, initial training students and tutors seems to be an obvious way of capitalising on resources to mutual benefit. Focusing theorising on pupils' learning in the classroom and developing skills to evaluate it systematically are not only professionally appropriate but also invest the adults' learning with the sharp edge of necessity. 'Does it improve the children's learning?' becomes a question requiring an answer and not a matter of leisurely speculation.

It seems unarguable that there should be a coherence of purpose across children's total curriculum experience. This can only be achieved by collaboration in planning and in evaluation - given the demands on teachers' time, that collaboration has to be sophisticated and efficient. Teacher education must surely concern itself with the teacher's role beyond the classroom and subject. Opportunities to experience and to gain skills for serving a common purpose with colleagues, sharing tasks, and providing and accepting expertise would seem to be essential.

IT-INSET encapsulates the above propositions in a classroom-based programme in which teachers, students and tutors combine to evaluate and develop the learning of pupils. The professional relevance of this concept is best illustrated in the words of one headteacher:

> IT-INSET adds a useful extra dimension to staff and curriculum development. It offers us the opportunity to work collaboratively with people with fresh ideas and perspectives to be examined in a situation that demands that we, in turn, justify, clarify and modify our own ideas and practice. In IT-INSET we all learn from each other in a climate which is at the same time demanding and supportive.

> We have found that, through building into the project design a weekly discussion component for our whole staff plus tutor and students, we bring into sharper focus issues of progression and continuity which are important in all areas of learning. IT-INSET has the particular benefit of giving teachers experience of taking on the roles of observer and evaluator in their own classes which offers them new insights into children's learning.

> When 'the project' itself is over, we are left with further questions that we want to explore and thus it provides an excellent basis for further in-school development.

The quality of current IT-INSET practice

It has been argued that teachers inevitably theorise. It can also be taken for granted that teachers enjoy a large measure of social competence. Indeed, social skills figure prominently in the Secretary of State's list of personal qualities that should be manifest in candidates accepted for initial training. They should have: 'A sense of responsibility, a robust but balanced outlook, awareness, sensitivity, enthusiasm and facility in communication' (DES 1984). Given these two sets of attributes, cognitive and social, it follows that all teachers, students and tutors should be capable of engaging in IT-INSET with some measure of success. They begin with the relevant attributes and the function of the programme should be to refine and sharpen them so that they better serve the participants' teaching purposes.

Most of the institutions involved are striving to establish IT-INSET programmes designed to develop student, teacher and tutor skills for theorising and collaboration. A small number are employing the IT-INSET label for programmes with different intentions, usually those of mini-teaching practices. Even among those committed to genuine IT-INSET, achievements vary, as has been shown earlier. In general, however, the most typically successful elements of IT-INSET programmes, in the eyes of the participants themselves and of those who have studied them, are the observation of pupils' learning together with some degree of analysis, the making of improvements in details of curriculum provision and, above all, in working as collaborating teams. The consideration of 'external theory' is very uneven across institutions.

Teams are typically rather less successful in focusing progressively upon the pupils' learning under consideration, attempting to assess it, reconsidering its value and re-examining the curriculum provision which gives rise to it. In other words, their observations and analyses of learning tend not to be co-ordinated into an evaluation of the relevant aspect of the curriculum. As a consequence, few teams engage in developing the curriculum in other than minor ways. Almost all IT-INSET is classroom-bound and rarely are staff colleagues involved in any way. When other staff members do take an interest in an IT-INSET programme, by visiting the classroom or discussing it at a staff meeting, this has almost invariably been organised by the headteacher. Teams tend to respond to staff interest but rarely to initiate it.

The point at issue, then, is why the component activities of IT-INSET, which lie within the competence of all students, teachers and tutors, are not better and more consistently developed.

The nature and source of problems in IT-INSET

Taking all of the evidence into account, three areas of difficulty seem most to inhibit successful practice in IT-INSET. The first is that of communication of its philosophy and practice. Misunderstandings and partial understandings abound between all participants in all agencies - local education authorities, training institutions and schools. The consequences are all kinds of mismatches of expectations of IT-INSET.

The second area of difficulty is that of time. Almost universally, participants suffer from a lack of time to prepare for programmes, both before they begin and while they are in progress. Programmes are often too short to allow team members to do more than begin the process. IT-INSET demands sustained thought at all stages and the development of relationships between participants which enable those thoughts to be exchanged. Neither process can be hurried, yet team members are invariably under time pressure from first hearing about IT-INSET until the end of their programme.

The third set of problems with which most team members have to contend is that of the lack of relevant skills. On the whole, participants embark on IT-INSET with limited, if any, skills for observation, analysis, evaluation, discussion, or working effectively together.

These three sets of problems - communication, lack of time and lack of skills - have a common root in the mismatch between the philosophy of teacher education which underpins IT-INSET and that manifested by some local education authorities, training institutions and schools. Communication problems exist when the concept of IT-INSET is unfamiliar and different from concurrent experience. Time problems exist when local education authorities, training institutions and schools do not place a high priority on collaborative, systematic evaluation of pupil learning, relative to other forms of teacher education. Skills are lacking when they are not considered essential - and thus are not developed - in other areas of initial and in-service education. Where the match of philosophy between existing provision and IT-INSET has been closer, the problems have undoubtedly been fewer.

The choice for local education authorities, training institutions and schools

IT-INSET has been practised for ten years although its history for most individual local education authorities, training institutions and schools is very much shorter. At the outset, IT-INSET had the status of a national project funded by the Department of Education and Science and continued until 1988 to be supported by the Department. It received a further boost when the Secretary of State published criteria for the approval of initial training courses and IT-INSET was seen to make an effective contribution to meeting some of those criteria. This interpretation was underlined in *CATENOTE 4* (CATE 1986) when IT-INSET was specifically named as an appropriate example of the required partnership between schools and training institutions.

Motives for adopting IT-INSET have inevitably been very mixed. They vary from the wish to be identified with a national initiative, through attraction to some elements of the process, to deeply felt commitment to the philosophy of teacher education which IT-INSET represents. Experience of the last ten years suggests that local education authorities, training institutions and schools have three options in respect of IT-INSET.

1. They can reject IT-INSET as incompatible with their current philosophy and practice.

2. They can accept IT-INSET as a limited element in their provision which provides some experience of collaborative study of children's learning, which will provide modest but useful outcomes for the pupils and team members, and which may, or may not, develop more fully in the course of time.

3. They can accept IT-INSET as an inevitable expression of their teacher education philosophy and seek to bring their practice across the board in line with their philosophy and, in so doing, reduce the difficulties currently inherent in mounting IT-INSET programmes.

Option 3 represents a major decision. Nevertheless, it has already been taken by some local education authorities and training institutions. There are two initial issues for consideration by all those choosing to adopt Option 3 fully and to review their teacher education practice in the light of that decision. One concerns the partnership between local education authorities and training institutions and the other is a matter of timescale.

Collaboration between local education authorities and training institutions

First, since both initial and in-service education are concerned in IT-INSET, and since IT-INSET is grounded on a broader premise of continuity of learning through all phases of teacher education, progress cannot be made without close collaboration between local education authorities and training institutions and between both of these and schools.

Continuing discussions are essential to establishing progressively a shared philosophy and approach. Occasional meetings between advisers and tutors to agree on which schools will be invited to participate are far from sufficient for creating a foundation of common understandings and purposes.

Second, it may be that the practical implications of collaboration between local education authorities and training institutions need to be explored and the allocation of resources re-examined. Perhaps the case for practical local education authority support is best made by headteachers. The first comes from an infant school:

> The work of IT-INSET, its role within our school and our involvement with it was discussed in school by all staff. Together we discussed our school's priorities with regard to the curriculum. Play was a topic the majority of staff wished to explore further as we believed our curriculum could be built around it provided we were aware of opportunities and progression. ... I was amazed at the interest displayed by the staff not directly involved in the work of the IT-INSET group. Play became the focal point of our staffroom. Staff wanted to be involved. This pleases me as all, bar one, of the staff have been teaching a very long time and at this school for a long time too. The presence of the IT-INSET group motivated the staff to appraise their views on play and how they were using it in the classroom. It encouraged some of them to evaluate their methods of teaching. Classrooms have been reorganised and visits have been undertaken - two things I have been trying to encourage since I came to this school. My

assessment of IT-INSET is very favourable. It has helped my staff to clarify their views, in some cases to change their attitudes and to apply their new knowledge. The staff would like the input of IT-INSET again as it stimulates interest, argument and evaluation. The input of IT-INSET presents a motivating challenge to a highly experienced, long-serving but responsive staff.

Comments from other headteachers make similar points:

It is one of the factors we see leading to classroom-focused INSET and a deeper awareness of learning processes and their qualititative aspects. *(11-18 Community College)*

There has been a considerable amount of in-service and personal development for the members of staff who have participated and it has certainly changed the teaching style in one subject area for one particular year group. Other staff have shown considerable interest in what has been happening and are giving thought to their own departments but, as of now, there have been no major new initiatives. Many feel that with profiling and extension of the Technical and Vocational Education Initiative around the corner they have enough on their plates and have yet fully to realise that much of the approach used within the IT-INSET area has relevance to such initiatives. *(11-18 Comprehensive)*

IT-INSET has undoubtedly proved a tool for change in mathematics. The emphasis moved from didactic teaching approaches to facilitating learning, based on the regular opportunity to sit together in a team and analyse the last session and plan the next, concentrating on the process of learning. *(11-18 Community College)*

I feel that IT-INSET gave the opportunity to look closely at an area of teachers' concern. It is seldom that a teacher in school gets the opportunity to stand back and observe the children, then discuss and compare those observations. This is not only beneficial for the students but also for the teacher concerned and in turn for other staff within the school. Through the use of a questionnaire, other staff were involved and made to think about children's learning. The final written paper is a useful document that can be shared by staff and built upon by those concerned, long after the students have left the school. *(9-13 Middle School)*

The staff involved in the teams here were encouraged to examine their work from the viewpoint of the children in their classes. Their attention was focused more directly on the experience of the child and they examined more closely and critically their teaching strategies and material. *(10-14 High School)*

If local education authorities place value upon this kind of contribution to the development of their schools, then it may be that two particular funding issues need to be examined.

First, if teachers are to benefit to the full, those directly involved need to be able to play a full part in the weekly evaluation and planning discussions of the team. There is an urgent need for supply cover and a consequent redistribution of the funds from Grant-Related In-Service Training to support this kind of classroom-based evaluation. This can be achieved through establishing the assessment and evaluation of pupil learning as a local priority or by using IT-INSET as one form of training required by the Local Education Authority Training Grants Scheme (DES 1986).

Second, while IT-INSET benefits all participants, and students and tutors gain in company with teachers and schools, the costs of IT-INSET do fall unequally (Goulden 1986). Travel to schools in which students and tutors would not normally work on the grounds of distance, and for possibly longer periods, places an extra financial burden upon training institutions. Similarly, the staffing of IT-INSET places acute strain on institutional resources both in depleting staff available for other areas of the course and sometimes in employing part-time tutors for the purpose. The contribution to INSET which IT-INSET represents is a new feature of initial training courses and perhaps its practical implications need to be more fully considered in the way that is beginning to happen in a small number of the local education authorities involved.

The timescale for development

The philosophy of teacher education of which IT-INSET is one expression frequently requires for its practice fundamental changes in adviser and tutor teaching styles, attitudes, definitions of professional knowledge, roles and relationships. Such changes are not accomplished quickly and all parties to IT-INSET and related developments in teacher education need to work to a much longer time perspective.

There seems to be an expectation that IT-INSET will be implemented successfully on the first occasion and, at worst, the second. If there is commitment to the model of the teacher as a practical theoriser, and to the attendant concept of the role of collaboration in learning, there needs to be a long timescale of progressive change in teacher education. Some of these changes can be considered in relation to the particular difficulties referred to above that have emerged in implementing IT-INSET successfully - problems of communication, time and lack of skills.

Problems of communication

The concept of IT-INSET is constantly being communicated by those with some understanding and experience of it to those with little or none. After the initial transmission from the Centre for Evaluation and Development in Teacher Education to local education authorities and training institutions, the message is retransmitted to tutors, students, headteachers, and teachers. Even though advisers and tutors build up their own stock of understanding and experience, year by year they convey the IT-INSET concept to those meeting it for the first time. Every new group of 'receivers' can only bring their past and concurrent experience - and their interpretations of those - to bear upon what they are told. Definitions and explanations of IT-INSET are often abstract and inevitably newcomers clothe concepts such as 'collaboration', 'evaluation', 'developing pupils' learning', 'observation', and 'discussion' with meanings that they have had for them hitherto.

Sometimes the match between IT-INSET and previous experience is close and newcomers take for granted that, for example, observation means the purposeful and systematic gathering of data, developing pupils' learning means changing curriculum experiences in the light of pupils' assessed capabilities and difficulties, discussion means an organised exploration of emergent issues, and collaboration means subscribing to a shared purpose and valuing, but critically assessing, everyone's contribution to that purpose. Sometimes the match with previous experience is not so close and, at worst, observation means unplanned looking, developing pupils' learning means importing new ideas into the classroom without regard to their appropriateness for the particular pupils, discussion means either a casual chat or listening to the tutor, and collaboration means working together to implement the teacher's or tutor's ideas.

On the whole, communication of the IT-INSET concept is improving as those involved experiment with a variety of means. Not surprisingly, the more successful means incorporate some form of demonstration of the ideas involved. Videos of teams in action have been found to be helpful, for example, together with team reports in which participants describe and analyse their experience in language which evokes appropriate images in the minds of colleagues.

A particularly powerful means of communication is that of enabling future participants to observe and discuss IT-INSET in operation with colleagues in their own or other institutions. So far, such opportunities have been mainly available to the teachers seconded to evaluate IT-INSET, who have played an important role in dissemination in their own local education authorities.

Participants report that the documentation provided by the Centre for Evaluation and Development in Teacher Education has improved in clarity of explanation, though while generally available it has not always been widely circulated. Local education authorities and training institutions are increasingly preparing their own material (e.g. Everton, undated; Platt 1988). Generally, however, any kind of documentation has been found to be considerably more useful when it has been used as a basis for discussion of the ideas involved, rather than simply handed out.

Coming to terms with IT-INSET, and with the teacher education philosophy underpinning it, is not simply a matter of understanding the concepts involved. It also requires a willingness to accept its personal implications. Knowledge confers power, or at least provides a sense of security. Accepting someone else's knowledge is relatively undemanding; proving that it has been acquired provides a reassuring sense of success. If knowledge becomes problematic and is tested by its contribution to practical theorising, and if practical theorising is open to be tested for its logic, regard for evidence and justification, then all team members are at risk. The ground rules are changed and the easy retreats into superior status, greater knowledge and experience, on the one hand, and uncritical dependence, on the other, are cut off. For many students, teachers and tutors, this is an exciting liberation. For others, it is intolerably threatening and sometimes, for these reasons alone, IT-INSET is distorted into the practice of more familiar roles and processes.

In the long term, the most effective solution to these problems of communication of the IT-INSET concept will be to change practice in teacher education so that IT-INSET becomes less and less different from participants' previous experience. Such changes must be inevitable if local education authorities, training institutions and schools are genuinely committed to the teacher education philosophy that IT-INSET represents and are prepared to recognise that perhaps some of their present practice is implicitly underpinned by a different philosophy.

In significant ways, the time is appropriate for reconsidering modes of teaching and learning in teacher education. The Secretary of State's criteria seem to invite a new concept of educated teachers:

[Subject studies should be conducted] at a level appropriate to higher education.

Students should experience a wide range of teaching and learning methods and be given ample opportunity to discuss and assess them.

Opportunities should be provided for students to reflect on and learn from their own classroom experience, and to place their role as a teacher within the broader context of educational purposes.

Courses should ... pay attention to other aspects of the teacher's work, including the importance of staff collaboration in a collective professional approach to the curriculum ...

[Training] institutions, in co-operation with local education authorities and their advisers, should establish links with a number and variety of schools, and courses should be developed and run in close working partnership with those schools.

(DES 1984)

The Grant-Related In-Service Training arrangements place emphasis upon the role of teachers in identifying INSET needs and require that 'All training supported through this scheme should be monitored and evaluated by the [local education] authority to assess how far it has contributed to more effective and efficient delivery of the education service' (DES 1986). This appears to make pupil benefit the criterion of effective INSET and to recognise a prominent role for teachers in deciding on the kind of support that will best serve that end. Both sets of requirements can be seen to map on to a model of the teacher as a practical theoriser, an informed and rational thinker, focused on the evaluation and development of pupil learning and skilled in collaboration. These emphases can be used to create coherence between different elements in teacher education.

All teacher education is based upon a set of values, assumptions and propositions, even if sometimes they are implicit rather than otherwise. If these give rise to practice which mismatches with IT-INSET, and if those concerned endorse the philosophy of IT-INSET, then a stringent review of current practice is inescapable. The undisputed goal of teacher education must be to enhance the ability of teachers to enhance the learning of pupils. The extent to which the philosophy and practice of IT-INSET may contribute to this is available for inspection throughout this book. Teacher educators must decide, bearing in mind that little else in teacher education has been submitted to so extensive an evaluation.

Problems of time

IT-INSET programmes are costly in time for all participants. The classroom work and ensuing discussion cannot occupy less than half a day per week. All but a very few participants judge that a term - about ten half days - is barely sufficient to develop the basic processes of IT-INSET. The higher order activities of evaluating and developing the curriculum and involving other members of staff stand little chance of taking place in so short a time. There is also a need for time in parallel to the programme for participants to plan and prepare classroom work, analyse observation records and devise schedules, examine children's work, write up team discussions, and read.

On the whole, IT-INSET programmes are starved of time and yet, when the participants were asked to rate their teacher education experiences for their contribution in helping them cater appropriately for children's learning, students rated IT-INSET second only to teaching practice, tutors rated it highest, and teachers rated only residential short courses and full-time secondments higher. This must surely suggest a reconsideration of the distribution of time between other aspects of initial and in-service education and IT-INSET.

The allocation of time signals degrees of importance. This device has been used, for example, in the Secretary of States's criteria (DES 1984). Prescribed amounts of time do not, however, automatically imply particular modes of learning. Nevertheless, they are often treated as if they do and proposals are turned into unnecessary, and possibly unintended, strait-jackets. Reference has already been made to the requirement that, in the course of subject studies, 'Students should experience a wide range of teaching and learning methods.' The criteria further indicate that the course should include 'A combination of taught time, structured school experience and private study.' It is interesting that students rated 'private study' above 'college-based work in main academic subjects'. It is clear that, within the 'hourage' requirements, there is room for the development of modes of teaching and learning which might better fit the philosophy of teacher education which a training institution seems to have espoused in adopting IT-INSET. Increased opportunities for independent and collaborative learning are certainly more demanding of students but would provide an experience of learning more appropriate as a model for continuing, post-course learning.

Tutors, too, might spend their time more effectively in exploring emergent difficulties and questions with students than in delivering material which, in any case, is much more readily and constructively absorbed from the printed than the spoken word. Some training institutions are already moving in these directions and, while such changes do not necessarily create more time, they do create more flexibility.

A different use of school attachments, other than teaching practice, would create time. Such attachments might be much more productively spent in developing generic processes of theorising and evaluating than in content-bound 'application'. Such processes have to occur within substantive areas and so close attention to successive areas of the curriculum is not lost but merely used more effectively. It is also evident that this kind of experience tends to be preferred by students.

For local education authorities, creating time for teachers equates to the cost of supply cover. Perhaps it might be considered whether the value of classroom-based work, which is very difficult to exploit fully without provision of time free of class responsibilities, might justify some redistribution of INSET resources. At least one local education authority has established this by including IT-INSET as a local priority under the heading of 'classroom evaluation' within their Grant-Related In-Service Training arrangements. The case was made convincingly by one headteacher:

> The IT-INSET in school contributed to an upsurge in the confidence and enthusiasm of the teaching staff, even those not actively participating. I believe much of the value lay in the fact that the staff were working in their own school environment, with its limitations, and with their own pupils. They were not listening cynically to someone pontificating from on high. They were really involved, doing it themselves, and realising that they were more than adequate.

Almost every IT-INSET participant complains about lack of preparation time. There are two kinds of preparation. One concerns the general concepts and skills involved in IT-INSET. The need for this kind of preparation could disappear if the relevant concepts and skills became central to initial training and INSET courses rather than being peculiar to IT-INSET. The second kind of preparation is that which schools and teams need to undertake specifically for the programme that is to follow. Team members need to get to know each other, to establish ground rules, working procedures and specific purposes, and to identify resources. This, of course, is part of the programme, but given present timescales it is often half a term before teams are established and working well. This kind of preparation, improving understandings and skills for a specific, practical purpose, cannot be compensated for by abstract and detached team-building exercises and the like. It seems inescapable that IT-INSET programmes need to be longer and schools, training institutions and local education authorities must evaluate the products of IT-INSET in comparison with other aspects of initial and in-service training.

Problems of lack of skill

It is apparent from the evidence that team members tend to lack skills in observation, analysis, evaluation, working together, discussion and study. At the same time, it should be recognised that most IT-INSET programmes actually last for between five and ten days in total. It is surely significant that most team members develop the skills that they do and this suggests that students, teachers and tutors share considerable ability to accelerate their own development of skills when they need to. Nevertheless, IT-INSET programmes would certainly profit, in terms of benefit to pupils, if participants began with greater relevant experience and competence.

This range of shortcomings in team members perhaps testifies more than anything else to the mismatch between IT-INSET and current and previous teacher education experiences. If local education authorities and training institutions genuinely subscribe to the philosophy and theory of IT-INSET, how can it be that observing and analysing pupil learning, reviewing value judgements, engaging in organised, productive discussion, and working collaboratively are so novel? There must be room to reconsider whether the dominant model of student, teacher and tutor learning is consonant with the espoused philosophy. The prevalent experiences of teacher education must be:

- learning through systematic observation followed by reflection;
- critical examination of substantive and theoretical resources;
- data collection and analysis;
- exploration of value judgements and their criteria;
- constructive exchange of information and propositions;
- writing to inform and engage; and
- working collaboratively.

Those processes have social implications and can be undermined if traditional roles prevail. Advisers, tutors, teachers and students have to share regard for rational argument, appropriate evidence and the articulation of value judgements. The changed status of 'external theory' and experience, from established authority to examinable resource, inevitably changes roles and relationships. Advisers and tutors on the one hand, and students and teachers on the other, cease to be the knowledgeable and the ignorant and become joint learners each with access to different resources. If these concepts are to be more than rhetoric, given brief expression in the course of an IT-INSET programme, they must permeate INSET activities and initial training.

Evaluation and development of teacher education

Teacher education has inevitably been subject to a good deal of crisis management in recent years. Uncertainties, acute pressures and demands have been faced in a context of shrinking resources. Advisers and tutors alike have been personally stretched to an intolerable degree to maintain provision. In such a situation, priorities present themselves in terms of meeting the next deadline. Yet the opportunity must somehow be found to establish where the professional staff of a local education authority or training institution collectively stand on principle and philosophy. It would seem that the obligation cannot be avoided and it is one which headteachers, facing similar problems, are currently required to meet.

The role of senior management is crucial: probably only they can signal the high priority for such debate, create the time and legitimate the diversion of attention from the immediate to a reconsideration of the whole rationale of provision. Current teacher education practice has to be examined in terms of the learning to which it gives rise and the implicit values which underpin that learning. Those who have chosen to adopt IT-INSET have to examine the existence and extent of mismatch between the philosophy and practice of IT-INSET and the rest of their provision. Identifying mismatches and planning developments in practice, though a long-term commitment, need to be begun with urgency by training institutions and local education authority co-ordinators of Grant-Related In-Service Training alike.

Development plans must inevitably have a long timescale. Not only may some of the changes be substantial, but they also require an unprecedented degree of co-ordination between local education authorities, training institutions and schools. It must be accepted that progress will be slow, possibly erratic and often uncertain. Without an agreed value position, however, changes are likely to be inconsistent and retrograde and to fail to do justice to pupils, students and teachers.

Appendices

Appendix 1
Membership of the steering group

Alan Andrews	Essex Education Authority
Ron Arnold	HMI *(to 1986)*
Patricia Ashton	CEDTE, University of Leicester
Gordon Benfield	Westhill and Newman College
Brian Cruickshank	Leicestershire Education Authority
Cedric Cullingford	Oxford Polytechnic *(to 1985)*
Joan Cuming	Newman College
Mary Hallaway (Chair)	Trinity and All Saints' College
David Hellawell	City of Birmingham Polytechnic
Euan Henderson	The Open University
Sue Hilliam	Leeds Education Authority
Graham Impey	CEDTE, University of Leicester
John Isaac	Oxford Polytechnic *(from 1985)*
Tom Jeffery	Department of Education and Science *(to 1987)*
Ben Kerwood	Oxfordshire Education Authority
Margaret Mathieson	University of Lancaster
John Merritt	
Stan Miller	Birmingham Education Authority
Derek Mortimer	Suffolk College of Higher Education
Alan Peacock	CEDTE, University of Leicester
Ken Pritchard	West Sussex Education Authority *(from 1987)*
Adrian Shaw	Department of Education and Science *(from 1987)*
Mike Tomlinson	HMI *(from 1986)*
John Wyatt	West Sussex Institute of Higher Education

Appendix 2
Chief education officers' questionnaire

1. What procedure is used to decide which schools and which teachers should participate in IT-INSET?

2. What, if anything, do you believe has been gained by the teachers as a result of IT-INSET?

3. In what ways, if at all, has IT-INSET benefited the schools involved (beyond any personal development for the teachers in whose classes IT-INSET began)?

4. What form of direct contact, if any, has been made by members of your advisory team with the curriculum evaluation and development work in schools?

5. What effect has IT-INSET had on relationships between your Authority and the training institution in IT-INSET work generally?

6. What part has IT-INSET played in the overall INSET policy and programme of your Authority?

7. What hopes or plans does your Authority have for the continuation and development of IT-INSET?

Appendix 3
Training institution questionnaire

1. What considerations led to the adoption of IT-INSET by your Institution?

2. What preparations were made by the Institution before IT-INSET began?

3. What factors influence which students and which tutors participate in IT-INSET?

4. To what extent was it possible to accomodate IT-INSET within existing curricular and organisational arrangements for initial and in-service students?

5. What staffing constraints, qualitatative and quantitative, have been experienced in operating IT-INSET? (It would be helpful to indicate the way in which staffing inputs have been measured for institution accounting purposes.)

6. What changes in roles and relationships have been noted among the students, teachers and tutors?

7. To what extent and in what ways have the ideas of IT-INSET extended beyond those actually participating in the Institution?

8. What is your overall assessment of the contribution of IT-INSET to the initial and in-service training of teachers provided by your Institution?

9. How would you like to see IT-INSET work develop in your Institution in the future?

Appendix 4
Questionnaire for headteachers

The following five questions ask you to describe and assess IT-INSET at work in your school. As you reply to each question, would you please refer, as appropriate in your experience of IT-INSET, to:

- yourself;
- the teacher(s) directly involved with the tutor and students;
- the other teachers in the school;
- the work undertaken by the team(s) in the chosen areas of the curriculum?

1. What considerations led to the participation of your school in IT-INSET?

2. What preparations were made in the school before IT-INSET actually began?

3. What effects did IT-INSET have on the school while it was in progress?

4. What is your assessment of the contribution of IT-INSET to your school?

5. How would you like to see IT-INSET work develop in your school in the future?

Appendix 5
Team questionnaire

You will have already received and (hopefully!) begun to complete the National Evaluation workbook, which is a record of your individual progress in IT-INSET, and the benefits to you and the pupils. In evaluating the benefits of IT-INSET in so many different places, however, we also need to have a detailed picture of what IT-INSET is in practice.

So the purpose of this questionnaire is to describe in detail how each team operated during the IT-INSET programme. It covers four main aspects, namely Planning, Teaching/Observing, Discussion and Teamwork.

All questions can be answered simply by placing ticks ( ) in appropriate boxes. You are not expected to elaborate on answers, but if you feel it is essential to do so, please add any comments on the back.

Since the questionnaire is aimed at how teams operate, please discuss the questions within your team and then complete one questionnaire only per team. It is very important that you also complete the Identification Data on the back page, otherwise very little useful analysis will be possible. Individual names are not necessary, however, and no team will be identifiable in any subsequent report.

Completed questionnaires should be returned via the College IT-INSET Co-ordinator to Alan Peacock, at CEDTE.

1. Who was primarily responsible for the activities below? (Tick as many boxes as necessary)

	Determining the topic	Planning classroom work	Organising discussion	Making things run smoothly
Headteacher				
Department staff				
A group of teachers				
The class teacher				
College co-ordinator				
College tutor				
The team				
Nobody				
Don't know				

2. Which of the following detailed planning activities was undertaken by the team as a whole? (Tick <u>one</u> box in each row)

	(1) All of it	(2) Some of it	(3) None of it
Work for the class			
Work for a group			
Materials preparation			
What to observe			
What to discuss			

3. Did you srtart out with a scheme of work for the whole programme? (Tick yes or no)

(1) Yes		(2) No	

If NO, go on to question 6.

If YES:-
4. Who wrote it? (Tick all those involved)

Headteacher	
Class teacher	
Students	
Tutor	
Team effort	

5. Did you stick to your initial plan or modify it as you went along? (Tick one box only)

(1) Stuck to it entirely	
(2) Changed parts of it	
(3) Changed focus completely	

6. How often did you teach? (Tick one box on each row)

	(1) Every week	(2) Some weeks	(3) Never
The whole class			
A group of pupils			
An individual pupil			

7. How often were you freed from teaching in order to observe? (Tick one box in each row)

	(1) Every week	(2) Some weeks	(3) Never
The whole class			
A group of pupils			
An individual pupil			

8. Did you use structured observation?

(1) Yes		(2) No	

If NO, go on to question 10.

If YES:-

9. Which of the following ways of structuring observations did you use? (Tick one box in each row)

	(1) Always	(2) Sometimes	(3) Never
Team-made schedules			
College-made schedules			
CEDTE schedules			
The 'Six Questions'			
Other (specify)			

10. How much time, on average, did your team spend together on discussion each week? (Tick one box in each row)

	(1) None	(2) 0-15 mins	(3) 15-30 mins	(4) 30-60 mins	(5) Over 60 mins
Evaluation					
Planning					

11. Did you have an agenda for your team discussion? (Tick one box in each row)

	(1) Always	(2) Sometimes	(3) Never
Explicit/agreed agenda			
Implicit/taken for granted agenda			
Deliberately avoided agenda			

12. What did you do about roles within the team? (Tick one box in each row)

	(1) Never had one	(2) Sometimes had one	(3) Always same person	(4) Rotated round team
Agenda writer				
Discussion leader				
Chairperson				
Recorder/ secretary				

13. What did your discussion <u>mainly</u> focus on? (Tick the <u>main</u> box in each column)

	In the first weeks	In the last weeks
(1) What pupils did		
(2) What pupils learned		
(3) What teachers did		
(4) What we learned		
(5) Worthwhileness		
(6) No clear focus		

14. How and when did you discuss the aspects of IT-INSET listed below? Do you understand them now? (Tick as many boxes as necessary)

	Never	Before we began	As we went along	I am still uncertain about this aspect
Philosophy/purpose of IT-INSET				
Identifying topic				
Team roles				
Benefits to ourselves				

15.   How would you describe the interaction between members
       of your team by the end of the IT-INSET programme?
       (Tick one box in every row)

We all contributed ideas						Few of us contributed ideas
Atmosphere was tense						Atmosphere was relaxed
We stuck to our roles						Our roles were blurred
We were very hierarchical						We were very democratic
We were suspicious of each other						We trusted each other
We all had different purposes						We shared a common purpose
We learned little from each other						We learned a lot from each other
We analysed pupils' learning						We never analysed pupils' learning
We never analysed each other's teaching						We analysed each other's teaching
We were all equally committed						Some were much less committed than others
We met only in timetabled sessions						We met socially at other times

16. Which kinds of interaction dominated your discussions? (Tick one box in each <u>column</u>)

	In the first weeks	In the last weeks
(1) tutor-student		
(2) teacher-student		
(3) tutor-teacher		
(4) student-student		
(5) none of these		

17. To what extent do you feel that you achieved the following? (Tick one box in each row)

	(1) Fully	(2) Partly	(3) Not at all
Observing classroom practice			
Analysing practice/ applying theory			
Evaluating the curriculum			
Developing the curriculum			
Working as a team			
Involving others in the process			

Information for Identification

18.   Name of training institution ....

19.   Name of IT-INSET school ....

20.   Age range of pupils:

       1. Nursery/   2. Junior   3. Secondary
         infant

21.   Number of teams in your school ....

22.   Team code (where more than one team in school) ....

23.   LEA of school ....

24.   Number of people in team ....

25.   Number of weeks in IT-INSET programme ....

26.   Time when IT-INSET takes place:

1. Morning		2. Afternoon		3. All day	

Appendix 6
The diary

The purpose of IT-INSET is to improve children's learning by teams of teachers, students and tutors undertaking collaborative curriculum review in the classroom, thus contributing to the professional development of all team members.

The Centre for Evaluation and Development in Teacher Education is now undertaking a final evaluation of the extent to which IT-INSET achieves this aim. In order to do so, we need your help in obtaining a national picture of how everybody (pupils, students, teachers and tutors) has benefited.

Please complete all sections of this workbook and return it in whatever way has been arranged by your IT-INSET co-ordinator. If you are in any doubt, please return the workbook direct to CEDTE in Leicester.

In order to identify you for the purpose of data analysis we require the basic information below. You will not be identified by name in any report.

Name of college/institution ....

Name of IT-INSET school ....

LEA of IT-INSET school ....

Team code (where appropriate) ....

Teacher/student/tutor (delete as appropriate)

Age range of pupils involved ....

This is my first/second/third/fourth experience of IT-INSET (delete as appropriate)

Name (optional) ....

AT THE BEGINNING

What area of children's learning is your team investigating?

What do the children generally seem to understand and/or be able to do in that area?

What exceptions are there to that?

What, generally, does their attitude seem to be to that area of learning?

How certain do you feel about the accuracy of your statements above?

What kind of evidence have you for the statements you have made above?

AS YOU GO ALONG

<u>Week 1</u>   Date ....

Major action planned/taken to find out more about what
the children are learnng.

Major questions raised.

Reading done, resources used, others consulted.

Contacts made with Headteacher or other staff.

(A further two pages were provided for each of the following eleven weeks.)

AT THE END

What gains in understanding or skills have the children made generally?

What exceptions are there to that?

What is the children's attitude generally to that area of learning now?

What kind of evidence have you got for the statements made on the previous page?

In your considered opinion, what is the value of that area of learning for the children?

YOUR ASSESSMENT OF YOUR TEAM'S ACHIEVEMENTS

IT-INSET is intended to give teams the opportunity to work together, to study, and to develop children's learning in the chosen area.

Looking back now, how successful do you think your team has been in this?

(Please tick)

Very successful

Successful to some extent

Unsuccessful

For the sake of future teams,

What factors do you think HELPED your team?

What factors do you think HINDERED your team?

Appendix 7
Relative benefits questionnaires

Students' version

Please complete this sheet AT THE END of your IT-INSET programme.

Below are listed nine aspects of your college course which we would like you to compare. The names used here may not coincide with those used in your college. If you are in any doubt about the meaning of any category, please consult your tutor before completing the questionnaire.

In column A please indicate which of these you have experienced in your college course so far.

In column B rate each of the aspects of your college course on a scale from 1 (of no benefit whatsoever) to 6 (of maximum benefit) in terms of how they helped you as a teacher to cater appropriately for children's leaning.

Score 1-6

	A	B

College-based work

1. In main academic subject(s)

2. In content and method of school curriculum

3. In theories of teaching and learning

4. With children

5. Private study

School-based work

6. Observation

7. Block Teaching Practice

8. IT-INSET

9. Other (please specify)

Consider the benefits to you of IT-INSET in relation to the benefits of Teaching Practice. Please state:

(a) Up to THREE ways in which IT-INSET is more beneficial than Teaching Practice.

1.

2.

3.

(b) Up to THREE ways in which Teaching Practice is more beneficial than IT-INSET.

1.

2.

3.

Teachers' version

Please complete this sheet AT THE END of your IT-INSET programme.

Below are listed eight forms of in-service experience which we would like you to compare.

In column A please indicate which of these you have experienced in the last two academic years.

In column B rate each of the forms of in-service experience on a scale from 1 (of no benefit whatsoever) to 6 (of maximum benefit) in terms of how they helped you as a teacher to cater appropriately for children's learning.

In column C please indicate which of these alternatives are NOT in practice available to you at present, as far as you are aware.

Score 1 - 6

	A	B	C

In School

1. INSET activities run by teachers themselves
2. INSET organised by outside agency,
   e.g. adviser/college staff
3. IT-INSET

Out of School

4. After school course/teachers' centre meeting, etc.
5. Day course
6. Part-time extended course
7. Residential short course
8. Full-time secondment

Consider the benefits <u>to you</u> of IT-INSET in relation to the benefits of Supervising Teaching Practice.

Please state:

(a) Up to THREE ways in which <u>IT-INSET is more beneficial</u> than Supervising Teaching Practice.

1.

2.

3.

(b) Up to THREE ways in which <u>Supervising Teaching Practice is more beneficial</u> than IT-INSET.

1.

2.

3.

Appendices

Tutors' version

Please complete this sheet AT THE END of your IT-INSET programme.

Below are listed eight forms of school experience which we would like you to compare.

In column A please indicate which of these you have experienced in the last two academic years.

In column B rate each of the forms of school experience on a scale from 1 (of no benefit whatsoever) to 6 (of maximum benefit) in terms of how they helped you as a teacher to cater appropriately for children's learning. Please rate only those you have indicated in column A.

In column C please indicate which of these alternatives are NOT in practice available to you at present, as far as you are aware.

Score 1-6

	A	B	C
1. Teaching practice supervision			
2. Group practice/school-based INSET			
3. IT-INSET			
4. Consultancy/Research			
5. Block secondment			
6. Intermittent secondment			
7. School-based INSET course			
8. Other (please specify)			

Consider the benefits <u>to you</u> of IT-INSET in relation to the benefits of Supervising Teaching Practice.

Please state:

(a) Up to THREE ways in which <u>IT-INSET is more beneficial</u> than Supervising Teaching Practice.

1.

2.

3.

(b) Up to THREE ways in which <u>Supervising Teaching Practice is more beneficial</u> than IT-INSET.

1.

2.

3.

References

Alexander, R. J. (1984) 'Innovation and continuity in the initial teacher education curriculum', in R. J. Alexander, M. Craft and J. Lynch (eds) *Change in Teacher Education: Context and Provision since Robbins*, London: Holt, Rinehart and Winston, pp. 103-60.

Anning, A., (1986) '*Curriculum in action* in action', in D. Hustler, A. Cassidy and E. C. Cuff (eds) *Action Research in Classrooms and Schools*, London: Allen and Unwin, pp. 56-66.

Armstrong, M. (1980) *Closely Observed Children: The Diary of a Primary Classroom*, London: Writers and Readers.

Ashton, P. M. E., Henderson, E. S., Merritt, J. E. and Mortimer, D. J. (1983) *Teacher Education in the Classroom: Initial and In-service*, London: Croom Helm.

Brooke, J. M. (1986) *IT/INSET in Calderdale*, Metropolitan Borough of Calderdale, Education Department, mimeo.

CATE (1986) *Links between initial teacher training institutions and schools (CATENOTE No. 4)*, CATE, mimeo.

CEDTE (1985) *Talking in groups (CEDTE Occasional paper no. 34)*, University of Leicester School of Education, mimeo.

CEDTE (1986) *Evaluation of IT-INSET: Rationale and strategies (Steering Group paper 8/2)*, CEDTE, University of Leicester School of Education, mimeo.

CEDTE (1987) *Doing IT-INSET - Planning and preparation for IT-INSET: A report of a conference held at The College of Ripon and*

York St John, Friday, 7th November 1986, CEDTE, University of Leicester School of Education, mimeo.

Cumbria Education Committee (1986) *Mathematics 5-11 (Curriculum Paper Number Six)*, Cumbria Education Committee, mimeo.

Deakin University (1982) *The Action Research Reader*, Victoria: Deakin University Press.

DES (1978) *Primary Education in England: A Survey by HM Inspectors of Schools*, London: HMSO.

DES (1982) *Education 5 to 9: An Illustrative Survey of 80 First Schools in England*, London: HMSO.

DES (1983) *9-13 Middle Schools: An Illustrative Survey*, London: HMSO.

DES (1984) *Initial Teacher Training: Approval of Courses (Circular 3/84)*, London: DES.

DES (1985) *Education 8 to 12 in Combined and Middle Schools: An HMI Survey*, London: HMSO.

DES (1986) *Local Education Authority Training Grants Scheme: Financial Year 1987-88 (Circular 6/86)*, London: DES.

DES (1987a) *LEA Training Grants Scheme - Monitoring and Evaluation: Note by the DES*, London: DES.

DES (1987b) *The National Curriculum 5-16: A Consultation Document*, London: DES and Welsh Office.

DES (1987c) *Quality in Schools: The Initial Training of Teachers - An HMI Survey*, London: HMSO.

Ebbutt, D. (1985) 'Educational action research: Some general concerns and specific quibbles', in R. G. Burgess (ed.) *Issues in Educational Research: Qualitative Methods*, London: Falmer Press, pp. 152-74.

Elliott, J. (1985) 'Facilitating action research in schools: Some dilemmas', in R. G. Burgess (ed.) *Field Methods in the Study of Education*, London: Falmer Press, pp. 235-62.

Everton, T. (undated) *The organisation of IT-INSET in Leicestershire*, CEDTE, University of Leicester School of Education, mimeo.

Gelsthorpe, T. (1986) *IT-INSET in Leicestershire schools and colleges*, Leicestershire Education Committee, mimeo.

Goulden, R. (1986) *Costs and benefits: IT-INSET in Calderdale primary schools, 1986 (CEDTE Occasional paper no. 38)*, University of Leicester School of Education, mimeo.

Halkes, R. (1986) 'Teacher thinking: A promising perspective into educational processes', *Journal of Curriculum Studies* 18, 2: pp. 211-14.

Harlen, W., Darwin, A. and Murphy, M. (1977) *Match and Mismatch: Raising Questions*, London: Oliver and Boyd.

Holly, P., James, T. and Young, J. (1987) *The Experience of TRIST: Practitioners' Views of INSET and Recommendations for the Future*, London: MSC.

Hustler, D., Cassidy, A. and Cuff, E. C. (1986) *Action Research in Classrooms and Schools*, London: Allen and Unwin.

Koziol, S. M. and Burns, P. (1986) 'Teachers' accuracy in self-reporting about instructional practices using a focused self-report inventory', *Journal of Educational Research* 79, 4: pp. 205-9.

Marsh, C. (1986) 'IT-INSET: A panacea for the 1980s?', *Journal of Curriculum Studies* 18, 4: pp. 449-53.

Nind, J. (1986) 'An enquiry into pupil-responses to non-literal art objects: A CRISES case study', in D. Hustler, A. Cassidy and E. C. Cuff (eds) *Action Research in Classrooms and Schools*, London: Allen and Unwin, pp. 87-94.

References

Nixon, J. (1981) *A Teachers' Guide to Action Research: Evaluation, Enquiry and Development in the Classroom*, London: Grant McIntyre.

Open University (1973) *Language and Learning*, Bletchley: Open University Press.

Open University (1980) *Curriculum in Action: An Approach to Evaluation*, Milton Keynes: Open University Press.

Peacock, A. (1985) *Initial thoughts about evaluation of IT-INSET programmes*, CEDTE, University of Leicester School of Education, mimeo.

Peacock, A. (1986) *Initial trainees' perceptions of the benefits of IT-INSET in relation to other aspects of their courses: A pilot study*, CEDTE, University of Leicester School of Education, mimeo.

Platt, H. G. (1988) *Issues in IT-INSET*, CEDTE, University of Leicester School of Education, mimeo.

Rowland, S. (1984) *The Enquiring Classroom: An Introduction to Children's Learning*, London: Falmer Press.

Sewell, G. (1987) *The teacher as learner: The whole school approach - An IT-INSET programme in Seaton Junior School, 1986 (CEDTE Occasional paper no. 40)*, University of Leicester School of Education, mimeo.

Smyth, W. J. (1984) 'Teachers as collaborative learners in clinical supervision: A state-of-the-art review', *Journal of Education for Teaching* 10, 1: pp. 24-38.

Stenhouse, L. (1975) *An Introduction to Curriculum Research and Development*, London: Heinemann.

Tickle, L. (1987) *Learning Teaching, Teaching Teaching... A Study of Partnership in Teacher Education*, London: Falmer Press.